The Parish Church?

Explorations in the Relationship of the Church and the World

Edited by
GILES ECCLESTONE

Contributors
LESSLIE NEWBIGIN
DAVID MARTIN
CLIFFORD LONGLEY
HELEN OPPENHEIMER
RUTH ETCHELLS
JOHN TILLER
PETER SELBY
WESLEY CARR
JOHN TAYLOR

MOWBRAY
LONDON & OXFORD

Copyright © The Grubb Institute 1988

First published 1988
by A.R. Mowbray & Co. Ltd,
Saint Thomas House, Becket Street,
Oxford, OX1 1SJ

Typeset by Getset Ltd, Eynsham, Oxford
Printed in Great Britain by Biddles Ltd, Guildford

British Library Cataloguing in Publication Data

The Parish Church?
  1. Church of England. Parish churches.
  Role in society
  I. Ecclestone, Giles
  261.1

  ISBN 0-264-67143-0

CONTENTS

Foreword

by the Archbishop of York, Dr John Habgood

This is the first major religious study mounted by the Centre for Explorations in Social Concern. The list of contributors should by itself give confidence that it is a serious and important exercise.

The Centre is an offshoot of the Grubb Institute, intended to have greater flexibility than the Institute in the range of topics which it tackles. It shares the same basic philosophy and methods, and the starting-point of this particular study is the understanding of the social role of religion developed by Bruce Reed in his book *The Dynamics of Religion*. Not all the authors share this understanding, so on one level the book can be read as a useful criticism of, and commentary on, the underlying premises. Some of the criticisms are conceptual, as in Peter Selby's essay, some theological, as exemplified by Ruth Etchells, and some experiential, as described by John Tiller.

The question addressed by the author, 'Does Society still need the Parish Church?', is one which church leaders at all levels ask themselves with differing degrees of anguish and puzzlement. Those who turn to this book for an answer will find a hardhitting discussion with no simple conclusion. The discussion centres on the contrast between the communal and the associational models of the Church, but most of the essayists refuse to make this an absolute distinction. All are committed to some kind of communal role, but there are wide divergencies on how this is to be expressed in practice.

At this time when there is much talk about the Church of England developing sectarian tendencies, there is great need for some clear thinking about what such tendencies entail. There is also a need for the Church to be delivered from some of its own fantasies about itself, whether as 'the Church of the nation', or as a potent influence within a defined geographical area. At the same time, there is a need to rescue the truth contained in these self-images. This book can help in all three processes.

I do not agree with all of it. Indeed nobody could, without self-contradiction. I have always found great theological difficulties in accepting an associational type of religion, because I cannot make much sense of a God who is only concerned with the chosen few. But I recognize that on the level of Church policy there are serious issues at stake, and it may well be that different policies are appropriate in different social contexts.

But whatever our presuppositions, there is valuable food for thought within these pages. The Centre has made a promising start.

Preface

There has to be a better reason for producing another collection of essays than a desire to rush into print and the co-operation of a willing publisher. The group who have been responsible for this one believe they have at least two.

The first, and perhaps the more important, is that they believe that the issues which are addressed in the following pages, and the questions that are raised, are of particular significance. The mainstream Churches have been desperately trying to keep up with a society that seems to find them more and more irrelevant, and the more they try to adapt to the changes around them, the more irrelevant they seem. Twenty years ago, it was fashionable to talk of 'secularization' as the cause of the distress felt by those responsible for ecclesiastical policy in the face of what seemed a wholesale flight from institutional religion. But it seems clear now that far from becoming secular, society finds itself caught up more and more in forces that are not of its own making, forces that might be described as demonic, and are certainly irrational. Any society that has an astrologer on Breakfast Time TV and watches videos by the score which depict the occult in weird and wonderful forms, or that seems to worship gratuitous violence has not become secular. It is meeting its needs in another way. It may be that what is seen is evidence of the break-up of a culture which, after several centuries of domination and colonization, now finds that it has run out of steam. The world has seen this phenomenon before, and will doubtless see it again.

It was against this background that the Centre for Explorations in Social Concern was set up in the autumn of 1984, an auspicious year, by The Grubb Institute, an independent social research organization. The Centre aimed to provide space and opportunity for individuals and groups to stand back and think objectively about what was happening in society, in order to interpret their experience and decide on appropriate action. Perhaps out of that standing back, people would be able to identify the seeds of something new, out of which growth could emerge. The time is not for instant solutions, but rather for interpretation. Within this overall aim, one such group set out to explore the relation of Church and Society. One symbol of that relation, which had obviously been of significance in the past, was the idea of 'The Parish Church', which became the focus of the exploration. Was the Parish Church and what it stood for still a viable model of the relation of the Church and the Community? If it was no longer viable, but merely an anachronism, a pleasant feature of the fantasy that people have of an idyllic rural past, then what were the implications, both for the future of the Churches and, more importantly, for the Society in which those Churches found themselves?

The second reason for the publication of the results of this exploration is that the group decided from the beginning that it would work corporately, not only within itself, but also with others. It consisted of three members of The Grubb Institute and two men in the full-time employment of the Church of England, and represented a decade and a half of experience in working at the task of combining socio-psychological insights with theological ones. Everything the group wrote would continue to work at that boundary, and would be owned and acknowledged by the whole group. So the first person plural became more than a literary device; when we say 'we', we mean 'we'. But we also decided that this corporate model should apply equally to our method, and so we wrote an introductory paper with the title, 'What is a Parish Church?' and invited two other groups of people to join us in our explorations. The first of these was made up of what we described to ourselves as 'eminent persons', whom we invited to respond to the paper by addressing the second of these groups, members of a series of monthly day seminars held between November 1985 and July 1986. Those who came would reflect on the issues which had been raised for them by the speaker, within the context of the overall theme of the seminars, 'Does Society still need the Parish Church?'

The process over the nine months was therefore a complicated interaction between the Core Group, as we called ourselves, the speakers, and the members of the seminars. There were, on average, thirty-five of these at each seminar, the majority of whom were 'regulars', drawn from a wide geographical area. Two thirds were clergy and one third lay people. Everyone had a copy of the original paper; some of the speakers had read what their predecessors had said; members were able to obtain any contributions from the speakers that they might have missed, or wanted to read. Furthermore, members were invited to, and some did, contribute short papers of their own which were also circulated. In addition, there were two extra seminar days held, one in the middle and one at the end of the process.

The book is the result of that process of interaction. Part One consists of the Core Group's introductory discussion paper and a supplementary one produced later in the process. Part Two contains the responses made by the speakers. Their talks were recorded and transcribed and so were not prepared as literary pieces. They were addressed to a particular audience on a particular day and, although the asides have had to be edited out, are substantially as delivered. There has not been the usual long process of refinement and polishing. The temporal sequence of the talks has not been preserved. They appear in what seemed to us to be a more satisfactory order, which is in the nature of an exploration. Some events make sense only in the light of what follows, and so it seemed reasonable to place the talks where they would throw the most light on each other.

Part Three is a final contribution by the Core Group which does not try to tie up the loose ends but is rather a reflection on the whole process, pointing towards possible territory to be explored in the future. The contribution of the members was crucial. That it is not explicitly recorded is due partly to the difficulties of reproducing the record of the discussion, and partly to the nature of the exercise. It is, however, implicit in much of the final contribution from the Core Group. We want to thank them for persevering with us in the exploration, for at times we wondered whether we were going anywhere, or whether we were merely going round in circles.

The real justification for a book of this kind lies in whether, having completed it, the reader is prompted to consider the venture worthwhile and is prompted to join the exploration for her or himself. We describe what we aimed to do as, 'not primarily a matter of intellectual debate, but of opening up opportunities for clergy and people to examine their own experience'. This book will have value if it can inform and stimulate such examination for the reader.

The members of the core group are listed on p. 161.

PART I

1

Discussion Paper: What is a Parish Church?

The Core Group

The past twenty-five years have seen major changes in virtually every aspect of the life of the Churches. To take the Church of England, the changes have included liturgy, method of government, deployment of clergy, forms of ministry, the relation of clergy and laity and of Church and State. As yet, there is no sign of this movement abating. Indeed a recent monograph of Lesslie Newbigin looks forward to a period of forty years of theological reconstruction, the period for which the Tiller Report also offers a strategy.[1]

While this activity may be taken as a testimony to the Church's energy and renewal, it has a darker side of anguish and confused feelings. The blurring of traditional conceptions of roles and relationships has led to a sense of isolation and insecurity; unsettling what it means to belong to a Church, to believe and bear witness, to exercise ministry. The reality which many experience is less of being participants in a shared movement of renewal and reform as of being victims, caught up and overtaken by changes whose rationale and structure are unclear and whose effect is to remove supports without substituting a new sense of direction and purpose.

We believe the fundamental *theological* issue underlying all this shift and confusion is God, His nature and His purpose. What is to be believed about God and His relation to the world? And within that relation, what vision does the *Church* have of its function?

Stated in *sociological* rather than theological terms, the question is to do with how the Church manifests its task as an institution *of* society and *within* society. This question has become problematic because the context in which the Church exists is increasingly one of fragmentation. The idea of society as a living body and the idea of a common humanity whose members are members one of another, has been supplanted by a paradigm of individualism, where no one represents anyone but himself or herself, or at best his or her particular group or interest.

This paradigm of individualism, stemming ultimately from the Enlightenment, finds expression in all the institutions of our society, from the family to Parliament. As we see it, one of the main challenges facing the Church is to examine its own relation to this paradigm, a challenge also presented by Newbigin in his monograph.

This paper represents one attempt to meet that challenge. It does not try to provide solutions or map out a way ahead. Rather, our hope is that it will stimulate debate by offering a modest tool for exploring the situation from the inside and for reflecting on one's own experience within it. Perhaps out of exploration and reflection can flow new ways of living with this situation, adapting to it, modifying it or transforming it through one's own praxis.

'Parish' or 'Associational': two models of the local church

The term 'parish' was originally used by the Romans to describe an administrative unit of local government. The fathers of the Early Church accepted the territorial idea, and the church of the parish became the 'parish church'. This is how it was in England until comparatively recent times, when the word 'parish' largely disappeared from local government administration but was retained by the Church of England to designate a geographical area which was the responsibility of a particular church. With the growth of other denominations and the recognition of the Roman Catholic Church in England, each with their own territorial divisions and sub-divisions, or none at all, the original meaning of the words 'parish church' was lost. Nonetheless, the idea of the 'parish church' may still have significance in understanding the dynamics of the relation of a church to its community.

The theory was that the parish church was accountable for the spiritual well-being of the entire community living in the parish. This is still held by many clergy and people in the Church of England, whether the residents are Anglicans or not. The parish's responsibility is to look after the well-being of the people, and to the extent that this view can be sustained, there is no fundamental distinction between evangelism and social action. The Church sees the parish and people as one whole. In practice, things are often different. While the clergy reside in the parish and have laid upon them special responsibilities to the people living in the parish, the parish boundaries often have meaning only when deciding who can or cannot be baptized or married in the church. In many churches a proportion of the congregation, which may include the church officers, live outside the parish. Their authority to be parishioners comes from attendance at worship. It may seem therefore that it no longer makes sense to speak about a 'parish church', particularly at a time when it is argued that people belong to many different groups and communities gathered around work or leisure, leaving the one in which they live to become relatively less significant.

We believe the idea of 'parish church' does still make sense, not necessarily as a description of what is actually happening in the majority of self-styled parish churches, either urban, suburban or rural, but as an 'idea in the mind' which embodies a rich vein of thought and action, theological and scriptural, social and psychological, informing the practice of religion and its relatedness to society and to human beings in need. This idea stands over and against a quite different conception and tradition which we refer to as the 'associational church'. We believe that much of the current debate about ministry and mission and many of the uncertainties and concerns being voiced in different ways by clergy and people can be illuminated by thinking through these two models and their implications. While it is probably true that in England, the Church of England has in the past come closest to exemplifying the parish church model, with other denominations tending to the associational pattern, we believe the distinction exists within most denominations and that the processes we shall describe express a more universal tension between two modes of engagement of Church and Society. However, in what follows the focus is on the particular application of the two models in the context of the Church of England.

The local church in its community

Over a period of time, any local church will inevitably form its own distinctive character within the community, even though it celebrates a common liturgy with other local churches and shares the same form of church government. In ecclesiastical terminology, this character may be described within a spectrum ranging across anglo-catholic, middle-of-the-road, traditional, evangelical, 'congregational' and charismatic.

In itself, nothing in this description indicates whether any particular church is of the parish church or associational church type. The difference is shown in the way the community in the neighbourhood regards the church, its building and its members, and in the way in which clergy and congregation decide how to relate to the interest in the church expressed by that community.

Some churches will be barely conscious of their local community, neither will the community take much notice of the church. For example, the members assemble and disperse without any fuss and the ministers make little attempt to visit those who are not church attenders. Other churches, however, have an influence upon the community such that members of that community begin to consider the church as 'theirs', without any conscious decision to attend it or to make obvious use of it under normal circumstances. The church building and the fact of its presence provide a religious focus for them; and in times of need, relating to birth, marriage, illness and death, men and women who have hitherto shown no link with the church make demands on its ministries.

Where the interest from members of the local community in the church is welcomed by clergy and congregation primarily because they see it as offering potential for church growth, we can identify characteristics of the associational church. Where, on the other hand, this interest has the effect of drawing out the members of the congregation into a concern for ministry to all members of the community, individually and collectively, then we see signs of the parish church.

While the associational church may welcome members of the community to its activities, it will assess the effectiveness of its ministry largely by their willingness to attend church and to join it. The parish church will also be glad when such people become church members, but its major concern is to identify ways in which to show the community that it cares and is open to be approached by people about any issues which concern the health of the members of the community at large. The members of the parish church are acknowledging that they have an accountability to human beings because they are in need. Because it is concerned with its community environment, this type of local church can also be called the 'contextual church' or the 'communal church'.

These different relations between Church and Community can be fostered, neglected, discouraged or exploited. Succeeding generations of the same church may respond differently, but we believe that over time most churches develop a style which steers them into becoming either an associational church or a parish church. This style is independent of churchmanship, and its origins may depend upon the size, age and architectural beauty of the building, together with the quality of leadership of the clergy and the nature of their ministry. In our experience, the leadership of the clergy is generally followed by the congregation, and so a tradition builds up in the local church.

It is here that the parish boundary, or rather attitudes to the parish boundary, become significant. If it is seen solely as a way of assigning the pastoral ministries of clergy in relation to others, then it is purely operational. If, however, despite the fact that members of the congregation may come from anywhere, they see the parish boundary as a way of defining the extent of their accountability for the community around their local church, and if that is further expressed by the prayer of the congregation and the clergy, then it can become a powerful symbol of that accountability. (The ceremony of beating of the bounds, in urban no less than in rural parishes, may be interpreted as an expression of this.)

Projection in the associational and the parish church

The distinction we have made between an associational and a parish church is further illuminated by considering two concepts from psychodynamics and the study of group behaviour. In this section we discuss the bearing of the concept of 'projection' on the understanding of church life. In the following section we consider a further distinction between 'relationship' and 'relatedness'.

Projection is a mental activity whereby individuals and groups project aspects of themselves onto an 'other', whether a person, a sign, an idea, a role or an institution, in order to cope with some anxiety. For example, children project the caring aspect of themselves onto their mother to encourage her caring for them. Followers project their hopes onto leaders in order that they might gain the Promised Land. Sometimes people project the dark side of themselves on to others and turn them into scapegoats; this is one way of understanding the biblical text, 'he bore our sins in his body on the tree'.

Projection is basically an unconscious process but it can also be felt consciously as something people do to each other. This process is the outworking of a basic mental activity of 'splitting'. Where an individual is aware of the tension within of good and bad feelings and impulses, in order to relieve anxiety he or she splits these good and bad feelings and projects them outwards onto others. So the good or positive parts of oneself are projected onto those who can protect one — parents, friends, clergy or God: the bad or negative parts are projected onto those who are to be fought or rejected — enemies or the Devil.

Applying this to the church at the local level, we can say that where members of the community project their concern about the meaning of life and death onto the parish church, and the clergy and congregation willingly accept those projections, then a fruitful encounter can follow. But if the local church does not accept such projections, both 'good' and 'bad', positive and negative, then the church becomes increasingly cut off from its community. Taking account of this process sharpens the characterization of a church as 'associational' or 'parish', the dynamics of its internal life and its relatedness to its context.

(a)   Projection in the associational church

In associational churches the members project good aspects of themselves onto the group, and bad aspects of themselves outside the group. To that extent, the members will idealize their fellowship and there will be a strong pull towards defining an ideal type of Christian to which each is urged to conform. Bad or negative projections will be directed towards outside bodies and agencies. Whatever threatens the group will be deemed bad. More broadly, these negative projections are put onto the 'world' as the enemy of Christ and His Church, and this enmity becomes the stimulus for evangelism, to rescue men and women from the world and bring them into the shelter of the Church. Because such a hard line is drawn between the group and the world, it is difficult for individuals to raise genuine questions and doubts within the group, for to be different from the rest is to be under suspicion. Hence the group concentrates more and more upon what it considers to be the true teaching of the Scriptures or the Church, and is less inclined to receive instruction from anyone who does not agree with it.

There are many possible variations in the patterning of this process. There may be an emphasis on small groups within the Church, even at the expense of its regular services of worship, in which the unity of the group becomes an important issue and leadership is vested in someone with charisma, without need for formal sanction from church leadership. In a church in which the vitality of Christian fellowship is centred on the small group, meeting for example around Bible discussion or prayer, the structure of the local church itself will be seen largely in administrative terms. Aim and vision will be focused on the 'informal' church as the Body of Christ, comprising the groups and their individual members, whereas the 'formal' church is there to see things are done decently and in order. Except where there are special occasions, like a mission or an outreach programme, the local church as a whole is no longer the vital unit for ministry.

Alternatively, an associational church may be composed not of a series of small groups, but of people who have a similar outlook on life, or are from the same social class, or fall within a narrow age range and who share a very specific set of Christian beliefs. Usually this will form an eclectic congregation whose members come from other parishes because the teaching of the Church appeals to them. To use another expression, it is a 'gathered congregation' and may appear almost as a church *without* context, with little sense of relating with or ministering to the community outside as it is.

(b)   Projection in the parish church

The parish church deals with projection in a quite different way. The members of the congregation, who are interacting with the world outside in many places and at different levels and have many different experiences, will seek to present a view of Christ and His Church which comprehends the whole of that experience. Attention will be given to the quality of corporate worship, which in its design will seek to address the needs and aspirations of human beings at all levels and in all places. Because of this the parish church will be more open to ideas from outside the church, more ready to listen to advice. (Objections to the Alternative Service Book may be interpreted in this context as a reaction to the loss not only of rhythm and cadence, but also of a more universal, representative dimension.)

Members of a parish church will therefore see themselves much more in terms of the whole parish, as representatives rather than simply individuals. They will not feel they have to agree with each other on everything, and can tolerate differences. Whereas members of an associational church, as we have seen, tend to project their good parts onto the church and their bad parts onto the world, members of the parish church are encouraged to bring both their good and bad parts into the church itself, acknowledge their sinfulness and their brokenness in the service and feel real as they do so. In the liturgy they will tend to project their good parts onto the clergy while struggling with the bad parts in themselves, and it is up to the clergy to gain the skill and spiritual depth to use worship as a way of enabling the congregation to take back into themselves their good parts before they go into the world and return to their 'normal' lives. In this context, the importance of liturgy in the parish church, and the centrality of Holy Communion, is that they sustain the spiritual and psychological reality of this dynamic.

As a result of the need to find someone competent to handle these projections in the parish church, its members generally welcome the distinction between ordained clergy and themselves, not because of any difference as Christians, but because they have distinct *roles*. Clergy who manage this process with wisdom and spiritual understanding will encourage lay people at the same time to be *as* little children as they approach the throne of grace, *and* mature in Christ as they take on their ministry in the world.

There is, however, a crucial danger which must be noted. Because in the parish church the boundary between church membership and the community is blurred, the relation between parish and community can become so comfortable that the church loses its impulse to serve the community, and hence dilutes its mission. A parish church only avoids danger by constantly evaluating and monitoring the way it is relating to the community. If the relatedness between Church and community is enabling the parishioner to gain a deeper insight into the Christian faith through the way he or she serves the community, then the parish church will not be in danger of losing its sense of ministry. But if the parishioner, in serving the community, loses touch with the Christ within him or herself, and is absorbed by the values of that community, then the commitment to mission will fade. Thus this relatedness between Church and Community is an abiding tension at the heart of the parish church.

'Relationship' and 'relatedness'

In the previous paragraph we spoke of the 'relatedness' between Church and Community. We follow this usage, and distinguish it from 'relationship', in order to clarify a crucial distinction in the way 'relations' between people are understood and felt.

An associational church only sees relations in terms of *relationships*. The ministry and work of the Church is to foster relationships between people — hence the emphasis on small groups, because the large congregation 'makes it difficult to have real relationships'. The task of its clergy is through relationships to build up the Church, and the emphasis on evangelism is to create a relationship between Christ and the sinners. Service and account-ability to others is limited to those with whom it is possible to make a relationship, which is why responsibility for the com-munity at large is seen as too vague and impracticable.

Members of a parish church accept the value of relationship between people, but have a wider notion of relations, construed primarily in terms of 'relatedness'. For example, a newly appointed minister may have few relationships with the congregation, but he has a *relatedness* to everyone. He has a relatedness to all the people living in the parish whether or not they are aware of it. He symbolizes, not as an individual but in his role as priest, *their* sense of relatedness to the church, which may or may not be expressed by them through their interest in it and their projections onto it and to him. Similarly, a sinner may not have a relationship with God, but he has a relatedness to Him both by his creation and also because Christ died for him. The gift of faith is to rely on that relatedness, which results in a trusting relationship with God. The point of stressing relatedness is to show that there is something between the Church and the Community, between mankind and God whether or not they are aware of it. That this is central to the life of the Church is indicated by the apostolic injunction to pray for *all*, which goes well beyond praying for those with whom we enjoy relationships.

The awareness of the dimension of relatedness does not dimi-nish the value of relationships, but makes sense of exhortations to love one's enemy, to love one's neighbour. Because the Samaritan recognized his *relatedness* to the beaten up Jew, he was prepared to make a *relationship*. So relatedness, when reflected upon, enlarges our vision about others, activates love and accountability to strangers. A sense of relatedness is the acknowledgement that other people exist and that we are part of their existence. It enables us to see the place of the Church in the community in a new light.

The local church and the diocese

Whether a local church is associational or parish will affect not only its internal structures and its impact on the local community, but also its relation to the diocese. If the majority of churches are associational, the diocese need only be an administrative machine. It may seek support from the local churches to finance central administration and it may in turn provide ecclesiastical, theological, legal and synodical services to churches and central organizations, but it has no specific *spiritual* function. The associational church wants to be left alone to supply its own ministry from within, and may even view the diocese as a potential threat to its own internal control. The Bishop is seen as external to the local church, and his role is defined primarily in administrative terms, accountable to the machine to provide the necessary resources for the continuation and expansion of the local churches in the diocese. He is principally a symbol of the collective fellowship of a group of independent churches. In such circumstances, it is easy to understand how associational churches can come to feel constrained by the traditions of Anglican church practice, and function more like congregational churches of other protestant denominations.

Where the parish church predominates, on the other hand, the diocese has the potential to be more than a machine, to become a living organism. Certainly, the parish church sees the diocese as providing the conditions and resources for carrying out its ministry, but it sees more than that. It looks for some overseer who can advise it about its relations with the community and with society at large. It looks to the diocese to facilitate its activities by creating an appropriate context in which to function. This means in particular providing an ordained minister who can work with the projections of the worshippers and be himself resourced and supported pastorally by the diocese to do this. The self-understanding of the parish church therefore presupposes a wider organization and the role of someone who can offer leadership to that system as an expression of its own inner dynamic need.

The role of the Bishop

The Bishop as the symbol of the diocese is the obvious person to whom projections will be directed. He will receive the projections of the local church and its promise of abundant life. To the extent that he welcomes such projections he acknowledges a relatedness between himself and the members of the local churches scattered throughout the diocese. That relatedness forms the basis of his care and concern for the churches, and strengthens his ministry and prayers for them. By contrast, in churches where projection is only acceptable within the local congregation, churches of the associational type, then he will be a stranger and remote from those congregations; they will not direct positive projections towards him. In fact, if something goes wrong with the local church, they are likely rather to direct negative projections towards him — 'it's the fault of the diocese'.

However, just as at the local level the church which is marked out by the community for their projections needs to be conspicuous in one way or another, so for the Bishop to be the focus of projections from the churches, he needs to be prominent and clearly identifiable. In some dioceses this may be achieved by regular visitations and the taking of confirmations. The very title 'Bishop', with its aura of both social and religious status can support this role. If the Bishop fights shy of this 'status', or gets caught up in the administrative machine of the diocese, it will be difficult for this aspect of his role to be sustained.

Given this model, it is not only the projections of the church members which the Bishop receives. He also receives the projections, to a greater or lesser degree, of a fair proportion of the population of the area of the diocese. They look to him as the local community look to their vicar. If he is to be effective in offering leadership as a minister of the Gospel and a spokesman for the Church, he needs to be the focus for the positive projections, the hopes and longings of the population for a peaceful and just society and the promise for the future. This aspect of the leadership role is offered publicly by the Bishop in his participation in government and civic functions, and in his association with prominent citizens.

How a Bishop takes up his leadership role in a diocese will thus both affect and be affected by the prevalent models held within the local churches under his jurisdiction. For a Bishop who seeks to offer leadership on the 'parish church' model, there are particular tensions which relate to the fact that the diocese is both a focus for leadership and an administrative body. Negative projections are thus bound to be directed towards the Bishop as an administrative head, alongside the more positive projections onto him as representatives of the Church. Moreover, the general trend in this as in other societies to be suspicious of 'authority', puts the Bishop in the position of the marked man, vulnerable to accusations from the media if he acts ambiguously, while yet entrusted with the longings of those who look to him to be the voice proclaiming deliverance from their fears and confusions. To hold this tension, without withdrawal or defensiveness, requires a passionate belief in the office.

Some implications and questions

In setting out to distinguish these two models of the local church we stated our purpose as being to offer a tool for exploring the situation of the churches in Britain 'from the inside'. Although we are convinced that these models describe realities, we do not doubt that the situation in many local churches and dioceses is more complex, with various mixtures of associational and parish features. There are also some aspects of the models we have only touched on in passing, in particular their theological and scriptural dimension, which call for more extended treatment.

As we read the current situation, much of the concern of clergy and laity regarding what is happening in the Church reflects the tension between these models as different ways of conceiving and living the relatedness of Church and community. Traditionally, the parish model might be said to correspond in many respects to the ideal, at least of the Church of England. Increasingly, however, this model has come under fire. The loss of active church members and of ordinands, the weakening of local communities, the particular challenge of the inner cities, concern at the 'conservatism' which is an abiding risk of such a model, the increasing awareness of living in a pluralist society, have all combined to loosen its hold on the life and practice of clergy and people. The tendency of clergy to ignore their congregation when they address society, rather than to speak with and through their congregation as representatives of society, and the practice of some clergy of becoming involved in largely or wholly secular roles, together with the proliferation of sector ministries, are symptoms of this. Other countervailing but linked symptoms are the understanding in some churches of the ministry of laity as being exercised primarily in the Church rather than in the world, the decay of forms of worship and liturgy, the growth of elitist group activities, and the individualizing of belief and practices.

It is time to take stock and to examine the assumptions which underlie what is happening. In particular, how far is the *parish church* still a viable model of the relation of the Church and community? If it is not, what are the implications, both for the future of the churches, their forms of government and their corporate life, locally and nationally, and for the society in which the Church is embedded and to whose needs it ministers?

This 'taking stock' is not primarily a matter of intellectual debate, but of opening up opportunities for clergy and people to examine their own experience. What is presented here, we believe, will have value only in so far as it can inform such examination.

2

Supplementary Paper: Further Thoughts on 'Parish' and 'Associational'

The Core Group

It has in many ways proved misleading to use the term 'parish church' to describe the model of the church which is being contrasted with the 'associational' model. We would now prefer to use the term 'communal church', drawing out the implication that its distinctive feature is to be found in the way it relates to the community which is its environment, its context.

Given this definition, it is possible for a 'parish' church, that is, a church belonging to the parochial system of the Church of England, to be considered either 'communal' or 'associational', depending entirely on how it views the local community and on how the local community views it. Similarly, it is possible for a non-Anglican church to be either 'associational' or 'communal', either to adhere to the 'gathered' pattern which, for example, many free churches originally took up, or to move to a pattern in which it feels accountable for, and to the communities amongst which it exists. There are examples where the local non-Anglican church is the communal church, and the Anglican church is associational, though technically still called the 'parish church'.

There are a number of further comments on this distinction which we want to make.
– It is important to consider a particular church not only in its geographical but also in its ecclesiastical context. One church may adopt an associational model in response to a communal

17

model taken up by a neighbouring church, or vice versa. This is
one reason why it is misleading to assume that the communal
model is 'better than' or preferable to the associational.

— It is arguable that historically the seed-bed of the 'associational'
church has often been the inherent danger in the communal
church of so blurring the boundary between church membership and the community that the church merely comes to
endorse the community's values, or those of one or other
dominant social group. In that case, individuals within the
church may either begin to behave in an associational way,
challenging the assumptions that the church is making about
the boundary, or they may leave the church in favour of another
which is overtly associational, representing a different conception of spiritual values or social values or the relation between
the two. Particularly at moments of religious and cultural crisis
or change, it may well be that the Church needs both models to
co-exist, if it is to rediscover the heart of its mission in a
community, or a nation, or the world.

— It was said of the Tiller Report that it was seeking a strategy for a
communal church based on an associational theology. It may
also be true for many churches that they agree with the communal model but in fact work in an associational way. An almost
schizoid situation develops, in which the demands of the community are accepted at one level but deeply resented at another.
This tension lacks the creative dynamic which faces the communal church as it tries to come to terms with its acknowledged
vocation to be that part of the local community which accepts
Jesus as Lord, without setting itself up as a separate body over
and against its local community.

— It is worth exploring how far the communal and associational
models can exist within one church or one parish. It may be that
different congregations within one church may operate in
different ways, or that individuals within a church may bring
different assumptions to it. This could be one explanation of the
antipathy which exists between, for example, those who want
Matins, and those who want a Parish Communion. It may also be
that parishioners who do not regularly, or ever, attend church

still see a local church as representing them, as 'their' church, though members of the congregation do not. Here again the creative dynamic between Church and Community may be lost in mutual misunderstanding and mistrust. (An example at the national level would be the furore and unhappiness that followed the Falklands memorial service in St Paul's in 1982.)

– One way of expressing the distinction between 'communal' and 'associational' may be to consider whether a church believes that its task has been fulfilled only when everyone in an area has joined it, or whether it believes that it can fulfil its role by existing as the representative of the local community, praying for it and holding it up before God regardless of the statistics of its membership. When a local church prays, 'Forgive us our trespasses, as we forgive those who trespass against us', does the 'us' refer only to those who are in church, or does it refer to the whole of society?

– It is important to keep in mind that 'communal' and 'associational' are only two possible ways of describing what might be referred to as a church's particular way of 'being-in-the-world'. It may be that neither model is adequate to represent the actual relation now between Church and community as this is experienced in the life and work of men and women, both within and without the church. This can only be tested through examining with attention one's own experience, clerical or lay: in worship, in ministry and in one's daily interactions with others in the community. 'Communal' and 'associational' are merely tools which may help in this exploration. In the process one may be led to discover new paradigms for understanding that experience and its implications for the life and practice of the Church in society.

Representation

One of the ideas which is becoming increasingly difficult to hold onto in contemporary society is that of 'representation'. For example, MPs are seen more as delegates from their own local party than as representatives of their total constituency. (Perhaps the new re-selection procedures being applied in the major parties are an indication of this.) A delegate can express only the views of those who have delegated him or her; a representative can speak on behalf of others: he or she does not always have to go back for further instruction. The picture of a human being which is so often used now is that of the individual, bound by the confines of the body. I can speak only for myself and no-one else can speak for me. Another way of looking at a human being, one which in many ways accords more with the biblical picture, is as a person who carries around within him or herself complete worlds, populated by the people he or she meets and interacts with. A mother in this sense carries her family around inside her, and when you meet her, you also meet her family. Similarly, when she engages in an activity, she does so on behalf of the whole family. It is in this sense that we can truly represent others. We do things on behalf of others.

This distinction is obviously important when we consider worship. Do we worship as individuals or on behalf of others, as representatives? Do we carry with us into church the people and institutions with whom we have dealings, or do we leave them behind at the church door? It is difficult to understand what intercessory prayer is about without having some notion that we are in some way praying *on behalf of* others as well as *for* them. It is in this way that a local church can be representative of the local community, interceding for it, expressing its regret and sorrow for its sin, feeling one with it in its need and helplessness. It is in this way that it is possible to understand Christ as the representative person, one who bears the sin of the whole world, and through whom the whole world is redeemed.

Further Musings

— What does it mean to be a minister or a member of the congregation within these two models? Is either model truly adequate to that meaning?
— Does society have a need that the Church can answer? And what sort of church? Does the Church provide an external voice

which challenges the values of society, and stands for an objectivity outside society? And if it does, how does that relate to people's need for confirmation of their values in what has been called a 'tail-end society'? Is either possible in a pluralist multi-faith world?

— What sort of society is it that needs empty churches? Do we think God will be pleased if the churches are full? Or is it in their emptiness that the significance of God's word to us now will be found?

— Does the Church (and what kind of church) represent the interaction between the people of God and the nature of our society, and in that sense, as far as it does, is it creating both health in society and faith in Christ's body?

— Do we need to train clergy? Why not just ordain lay people? As soon as we train people, we change them. On the other hand, is there a value in the idea of the clergy as the 'resident stranger', who is *in* but not wholly *from* the community, a representative *of* them but also *to* them.

— We bring so many assumptions about the parish church to the discussion. How can we bring these to the surface?

— The theological doctrine of the Incarnation is trying to express the fact of the two natures of Christ; he was both God and man. Most of what came to be called heresies were expressions which failed to do justice to both. They overemphasized one or the other, or mixed them up. Do we have the same problem with the Church? How can it be both part of the fallen world and a foretaste of the world to come? If we emphasize the one, the Church merely conforms to the values of the world: if we emphasize the other, it rejects the world and projects all its own shortcomings into the world.

PART II

3

On Being the Church for the World

Lesslie Newbigin

The understanding of the Church found in the New Testament is essentially Christological. The Church exists for the world as Christ exists for the world, in judgement and in promise. It shares in the mission of Christ: 'as the Father sent me, so I send you'. As such, models of the Church which focus on the growth of the Church alone are ruled out, as are models which merely emphasize the meeting of human need or the achievement of particular human goals. Instead the Church is to be seen, and will rightly be judged, as a foretaste and instrument of God's Kingdom, offering an experience of the life of the Kingdom, while pointing beyond itself to a consummation beyond history. The major problem facing all churches today is the power of the denominational model, which colludes with the agnosticism of contemporary society concerning the truth claims of the Gospel, and allows churches to withdraw from the commission laid upon them, to be the Church of God for the places in which they are set.

I was ordained in the Church of Scotland for foreign missionary service. I went out with about eleven years of the old British Raj still to go, as an old-fashioned district missionary, monarch of all I surveyed and telling everybody else what to do, but not yet having really learned to do it myself. Then I became a Bishop of a diocese, with twelve years of very exciting experience in seeking to knit together two very different traditions, Anglican and Congregationalist — they put a Presbyterian in to keep the peace between the two! After that I became what I suppose one would call an ecumenical bureaucrat, after which I went back to India to the very different kind of role of being Bishop in Madras, an enormously expanding city.

Now, at the very end, I am beginning to learn what I ought to have learned at the beginning. I am the minister of a little United Reformed Church congregation in Birmingham. If you want to visit me you ask for Winson Green Prison and then look for the building just opposite, which Hitler unfortunately missed. That is where I try to minister. This is one of these typical inner-city areas where a demolition order was put on the church thirty-five years ago, which has neither been withdrawn nor carried out, and most of the houses round about and all the shops, have been knocked down. My congregation point to a field of thistles and say, 'That's where I was born and brought up', and the folk who have gradually been brought in are, as the local beat policeman said to me, all OHMS. I thought he was saying something about the prison, and said 'What exactly do you mean?' He said, 'Only Hindus, Muslims and Sikhs'. So we have this situation of a loyal congregation of white ageing people who, not of their own will, have been banished to the suburbs and do not have cars to travel in, trying to minister to a local area where it is not just thistles and tin cans but is mostly Hindus, Muslims and Sikhs. That is the sort of background out of which I shall try to speak.

I have a special interest in our topic, because in the days when I worked in Scotland as an SCM Secretary I was in close contact with George MacLeod, who recalled the Church of Scotland to the parish principle. The Church of Scotland has a much more dominant position in Scotland than the Church of England does in England and the concept of the parish has been able to exercise a much more dominant influence in Scotland than it has in England. Later when I was Bishop in Madras, where we had about 120 congregations in this exploding city of three million people, I was constantly facing the fact that, although these congregations were growing very rapidly (I often used to have to point out that while Our Lord promised to be present where two or three are gathered, He never made that promise for two or three thousand), they were associational congregations. They were not congregations who felt that, intrinsically, they were responsible for that bit of the city. Therefore, I spent a lot of my ten years as Bishop in Madras trying to hammer the parish principle into congregations which were very largely shaped by the associational perspective.

My second point is the need for clarity about criteria. Obviously, changing sociological and cultural conditions, the enormous and rapid changes that are taking place in our society, are relevant to the way that we understand our task. But I do most deeply believe (and I have tried to carry that belief out in many different situations), that when we are looking for guidance and renewal, we have fundamentally to go to the scriptures. We do so not in a sort of unintelligent and stupid way, just picking up odd texts, but with the faith by which the Church lives — that the character and the purpose of God is rendered apparent for us in the scriptures, and understood as we read them in the power of the Holy Spirit and in the fellowship of the whole Christian Church in all ages. I think it is important to say this, because all of our society, all of our thinking in the last two hundred years, has been dominated by the inductive principle: namely, that in trying to find our way what we do is to assemble all the facts and then, on the basis of all the facts, make some kind of theory about how we ought to go on.

The inductive principle, which has been so enormously creative in producing what we call a modern scientific world view, is a method which is of strictly limited application. It is not applicable to the question of our ultimate destiny because, in relation to our ultimate destiny, we shall not have all the data until the universe comes to a conclusion. We have to depend upon another kind of reasoning. The Church exists because God has revealed himself in the story of Israel, in the ministry and death and resurrection of Jesus Christ, and we are in the world as the bearers of a revelation of God's purpose for creation, and that is the only criterion, ultimately, by which we have to be guided. Obviously we have an enormous amount of discussion among ourselves about how we interpret the scriptures, about how we relate what is given to us in the scriptures to the new experiences that come to us as the world goes on its way. But we have to be quite unembarrassed and unambiguous about the fact that we find our ultimate criteria in that which has been given to us in revelation, which is not available by a process of observation and induction from the human situation as we see it.

In the New Testament, the Church is always and only designated by reference to two realities: one, God, God in Christ; and the other, the place where the Church is. And when, as we know from the Corinthian letters, the believers were forming themselves into groups involving another name ('I belong to Cephas, I belong to Paul, I belong to Apollos'), Paul is exceedingly tough in his dealing with them. He says 'You are carnal' — that is a very strong word but it is the appropriate word. Paul responds to that information by simply presenting to them again the Cross of Christ, in relation to which every other name is relativized. No other name can take the place that belongs alone to the name of Jesus Christ and, therefore, when believers propose to identify themselves with another name than that of the Lord Jesus Christ they are, as Paul said, 'carnal'. That is to say, they are falling back upon the flesh, upon *human* wisdom, power or spirituality, and they are therefore falling away from the Spirit, which is simply the life lived through what God has done finally and decisively in Jesus Christ. This is not incidental; it is fundamental.

Look at the interesting word which the New Testament writers use for the Church — *ekklesia theou*. There was a considerable number of words available in the contemporary vocabulary of that Hellenistic world to describe religious groups of people who were drawn together by a common quest for salvation under some kind of name, with some kind of discipline and with some kind of tradition of learning. There were a lot of Greek words for this, like *heranos*, *thiasos*, and so on, and the opponents of Christianity like Celsus constantly used those words to describe the Church. But in the first five centuries of the Christian Church you never find those words used. The Church never defines itself in the language that was used by these various religious groups that were composed of people in quest of salvation. They used only this word — *ekklesia*.

As you know, there are two words used in the Greek Old Testament to translate the congregation of God — there is the word *sunagogos* and the word *ekklesia*. The New Testament writers could have chosen either of those words; the word *sunagogos* was already the word used by the Jews in the Diaspora. But they chose this word *ekklesia*, which is the secular word for the assembly of all the citizens, to which every citizen is summoned and expected to attend, in which the business of the city is dealt with. Paul always used the word, all the New Testament writers use the word *ekklesia tou Theou*, the assembly of God; the assembly, in other words, to which all are summoned without exception. And they are summoned not by the town clerk, but by God — not by Peter, not by Apollos, not by Paul, but by God. And that is why you have this interesting fact that you can use the word 'Church' or 'Churches' indiscriminately. You can say the Churches in Asia, or the Church in Asia because, in a sense, it is one reality, it is the one God who is summoning all people, and therefore, whether it is simply that group that meets in Thessalonika or whether it is the whole reality in the whole world, it is the same reality. It is the Catholic Church. The local church is not a branch of something else: the local church *is* the Catholic Church. It is the *ekklesia tou Theou*, and Paul uses the most realistic language about it. Even when he has to tell them that they are sinners in all kinds of respects, they are nevertheless the *ekklesia tou Theou*, defined simply by the 'place' where they meet, and any other definition is ruled out. And in the subsequent history of the Church this principle has been carried on. The basic units of the Church — the parish, the diocese — were all determined by secular realities. And that is fundamental.

I remember a fascinating discussion among a group of Bishops about the proper size for a diocese. There were those who said that the size of the diocese must be determined by the number of people with whom a Bishop can have a real pastoral relation. And in passionate opposition to that, I remember hearing Ted Wickham saying, 'No, the size of the diocese must be determined by the size of the human community. The diocese must be that which represents the purpose of God for this human community, and for the pastoral care of its members. You have got to make the proper arrangements. But you cannot determine the size of the diocese by the internal needs of the Church. It must be determined by the secular reality for which the Church is there'. That has been fundamental right through the history of the Church, that the structural forms of the Church are determined by the secular reality, and not by the internal needs of the Church; and that I think is true to scripture.

The relation between the Church in a 'place' and the secular reality of that 'place' is intrinsic not extrinsic. It is not just that it happens to be located in that spot on the map. It is the Church of God *for that 'place'* and that is because the Church does not exist for itself but for God, and for the world which Jesus came to save. I once got into trouble after taking a confirmation service in one of those Madras churches which I think was more 'associational' than 'parish'. In the meeting of the Elders after the service I asked the naughty question, 'What is this church for?'. There was, of course, a long and embarrassed silence and then I received the answer, 'It caters to the needs of its members'. 'Then', I said 'it should be dissolved.' The Church does not exist for its members.

One possible definition of the Church which I think is worth thinking about, is that the Church is the provisional incorporation of humankind into Jesus Christ. Jesus Christ is the last Adam. All humankind is incorporated in Adam. We are all part of this natural human world. Jesus is the last Adam and the Church is the provisional incorporation of humankind into Christ. It is provisional in two senses: provisional in the sense that not all humankind is so incorporated; and provisional in the sense that those who are so incorporated are not yet fully conformed to the image of Christ. So the Church is a provisional body; it looks forward. It looks forward to the full formation of Christ in all its

members, to the growth of its members in holiness to the stature of
Jesus Christ. It also looks forward in the other sense, that it is only
the provisional incorporation of what is in God's intention the
whole of humanity.

That is however nonsense unless we deal with the actual
realities of humanity. In talking about the world you have to talk
about that segment of the world in which you are placed, and it is
in relation to that segment of the world in which you are placed
that the Church has to be recognizable as *for* that place. Certainly,
the geographical definition of that segment may not be the only
one that is relevant, although I think it is the fundamental one.
There can be other possible definitions of the 'place', but it is of
the very essence of the Church that it is *for* that place, for that
section of the world for which it has been made responsible. And
the 'for' has to be defined Christologically. In other words, the
Church is *for* that 'place' in a sense which is determined by the
sense in which Christ is *for* the world. Now, one would need to go
into a whole theology of the atonement to develop this, but
obviously Christ on his cross is in one sense totally identified with
the world, in another sense totally separated from the world. The
cross is the total identification of Jesus with the world in all its sin,
but in that identification the cross is the judgement of the world,
that which shows the gulf between God and his world, and we
must always, in every situation, be wrestling with both sides of this
reality: that the Church is *for* the world *against* the world; the
Church is *against* the world *for* the world. The Church is for the
human community in *that* place, *that* village, *that* city, *that* nation,
in the sense which is determined by the sense in which Christ is
for the world. And that must be the determining criterion at every
point.

I take, as a basic text, the Johannine version of the Great
Commission. Missionary thinking has often been distorted by the
fact that when people say 'The Great Commission', they always
mean Matthew 28:18-end. There are in fact three basic forms of
the Great Commission given to us. There is the Matthaean form.
There is the Lukan form in Acts 1:6-8, 'You shall receive power
when the Holy Spirit is come upon you and you shall be my

witnesses'. Here, the mission of the Church is seen as a kind of overflow of Pentecost, not as a command laid upon us, but as a gift given to us. And then there is the Johannine version (20:19-23), and I would like to take that as a kind of basic paradigm for our understanding. I have said that we must understand the sense in which the Church is for the place Christologically; here it is, spelt out with the greatest clarity. The disciples are huddled together in a room, withdrawing themselves from the world in fear of the world and then, as he had promised, Jesus is present in their midst. 'Where two or three have gathered together, there am I.' And immediately his command, is 'Open the doors, go out into the world. As the Father sent me, so I send you.' And that is the launching of the Church. The Church is a movement launched into the world in the same sense in which Jesus is sent into the world by the Father.

I have always been grateful for the fact that in my first diocese, which was a largely rural diocese, about half of our congregation had no buildings whatsoever. And so for my first twelve years as a Bishop I was normally conducting worship in the open street — all the services of the Church without exception. My picture of the Church formed in those years is deeply etched in my mind, the picture of a group of people sitting on the ground and a larger crowd of Hindus and Muslims and others standing around listening, watching, discussing; and, thank God, when one came back a few months later some of those would be in the group in the front. So you get the sense of the Church not as something drawn out of the world into a building, but the Church sent out into the world. And the operative word in our text is the word 'as': in the sentence, 'As the Father sent me, so I send you'.

Now that 'as' in a sense contains the whole crux of the question under discussion. The question is not, 'Does *society* need the parish church?', but 'Does *God* need the parish church?'. That is really the question we are wrestling with. And this 'as' contains the whole crux of the matter. How did the Father send the Son? Well, one could go back to that basic text in Mark 1:14, where Jesus comes into Galilee preaching the Gospel of God, the good news of God, and saying: 'The time is fulfilled, the Kingdom of

God is at hand, repent and believe the good news — believe the good news that I'm telling you'. Now, that is the announcement of a fact. It is news in the strictest sense of the word.

I used to get awfully tired of being asked the same question when I was a Bishop in India. My house in Madras was half-way between the airport and the city, so it was a wonderful place for ecumenical travellers to stop off and have lunch. And after lunch one always got the question, 'Are you optimistic or pessimistic about the future of the Church in India?', to which I had to develop the standard reply, which was, 'I believe that Jesus rose from the dead, and therefore the question doesn't arise'. In regard to a fact, one is not optimistic or pessimistic. One is believing or unbelieving. But in regard to a programme, you can be optimistic or pessimistic. We are deceived by the media who constantly suggest to us that the Church is a kind of good cause which we have to support, and if we don't support it, it's going to collapse. Yes, if it's a programme, then one can be optimistic or pessimistic. But about a 'fact', these are not the appropriate words. The question is, 'Do you believe or do you not?' Here is a fact, and of course it is not a religious fact. It does not belong to that little slot in *Time* magazine, between drama and sport, where religion is kept. It belongs to the opening section on world affairs. The Kingdom of God is at hand. The reign of God is at hand. In what sense is that news? It is not news to the Jews that God reigns. That is a fact that they have known for generations. What is new is that the reign of God is now a present reality, with which they have to come to terms. It is no longer a theological idea. It is no longer a vision in Heaven. It is no longer something in the distant future. It is now a reality with which they have to come to terms. But you cannot see it because you are facing the wrong way, you are looking in the wrong direction.

On one occasion I had to visit a village in Madras diocese which, like many of the villages, was miles from any road. In order to get to this village you had to cross a river and you could cross either at the north end or at the south end, and in their wisdom the congregation had decided that I was coming in at the south end. So they had a magnificent reception prepared, such as only a village congregation in India can prepare, with trumpets and drums and fireworks and garlands and fruit and everything you can think of. I came in at the other end and found a totally deserted village, which created a great crisis. I had to withdraw into the jungle and the whole village had to reorganize itself and face the other way, and then I appeared. Well now, that is what the word 'repent' means. It is a total U-turn of the mind. You are expecting something quite different from the reality that is coming upon you, and so you cannot see it.

When you have made the U-turn, it becomes possible to believe. And so there comes the call; 'Follow me', and Jesus calls Peter and Andrew and James and John. But the Kingdom is not obvious. There is the complaint: 'We don't see it. Where is it?' and so there are the parables and the 'mighty works' — the miracles. But finally, there is the final parable and the final miracle, which is the cross. Ultimately, the reign of God is present in the cross. And only to those who have been called as witnesses is the secret given that the cross is in fact not defeat but victory, that it is the victory of God over all the powers of this world. And therefore when Jesus said to them, 'As the Father sent me, so I send you', he showed them his hands and his side. In other words, the Church will be recognizable as the bearer of this mission on which the Father sent the Son and on which the Son sent the Church, in so far as the scars of the Passion are recognizable in its body. So you have that classic definition of mission, which has been so much ignored, in St Paul's letters, where he defines his apostolic mission as 'bearing in the body the dying of Jesus, that the life of Jesus might be manifest in our mortal flesh'.

I think we have often missed something by concentrating entirely on that Matthaean version which can produce the kind of triumphalist picture of the mission of the Church. Here, however, the Church is recognizable as the bearer of the Kingdom, the presence of the Kingdom, in so far as it is marked by the scars of the Passion. And the Passion of Jesus is not passive submission to evil, but the price paid for an active challenge to evil. The Passion is what the theologians call the Messianic tribulation, that which occurs at the frontier, where the reign of God challenges the rulers of this world. And that frontier runs right through the whole of human life and it is when the Church is at that frontier that it bears in its body both the marks of the Passion and the power of the risen life, of the Lord. And so then He immediately says 'Receive the Holy Spirit'. He gives to them the power of his risen life so that they may be the bearers of his reconciling work. 'Whosoever's sins you remit they are remitted, whosoever's sins you retain, they are retained.' The Church bears in its body the reconciling power of the atonement in so far as it is marked by the scars of the Passion, and it is therefore the bearer of the risen life. And, if you see the mission of the Church in that sense, then all this futile discussion between evangelism and social action disappears. It is a discussion which is irrelevant. It is meaningless when you see the mission of the Church in the terms that this Johannine passage offers. I suggest that its version of the Great Commission rules out three wrong ways of looking at the local church.

The first way is that which takes Church growth by itself as the criterion. Now I don't want to be unfair to the Church Growth school, because I know that they have been self-critical. My old friend Donald McGavran, who is the guru of the school, is perhaps a little less self-critical than he might be, but I know that the Church Growth school does try to get away from a kind of crude statistical measuring rod as the one criterion by which the Church is to be judged. Nevertheless, the main thrust of the Church Growth school is that the Church is there simply to make converts.

There you get the associational model neat. When you ask what is the purpose of making converts the answer is that they may make more converts, and when you ask what is the purpose of those further converts it is that they may make more converts. There is, in other words, an infinite regress. And, as we know from the medical analogy, the multiplication of cells unrelated to the purpose of the body is what we call cancer. That is a very hard thing to say, and I don't want to suggest that the folk who are in the Church Growth school are blind to these points. But I do think that there is a very sharp note of criticism that needs to be made against the idea that the Church exists simply to make more members, irrespective of that purpose for which the Father sent the Son into the world, which is that the presence of the reign of God might be a reality *now*.

The second way is the concept of the local church as simply the religious aspect of the local community, providing a focus for folk religion, but failing to confront people with the sharp call for radical conversion. This is perhaps a particular temptation for the established church. Remember, my background is Scotland, and I think the established church in Scotland is inclined to yield to that temptation even more than the established church in England. But it is *the* temptation for the established church. And one understands the power of it, the tremendously deep attachment that people have to their parish church, even though they would never under any circumstances go into it until the day of their funeral. I think this concept of folk religion is one The Grubb Institute has been interested in. It is one that certainly needs a good deal of analysis. Having lived most of my life in India, I am bound to say that much of what passes for religion here is just what in an Indian village we would call heathenism. But it is also mixed up with a lot of vestigial Christianity. It's a very complex mixture, this folk religion. One should certainly never be contemptuous of it, or despise it. One should always be on the look-out for the signals that it gives us of a recognition of realities beyond the visible world. But the New Testament is very clear that there is a radical repentance needed, a radical conversion, if one is to see the Kingdom of God.

Having said that, I want to say very strongly that conversion is the work of the Holy Spirit. Conversion is not something which can be programmed or accomplished or manipulated, even by the most expert evangelist. If there is one thing I have learnt as a missionary it is that though I was in a situation where, thank God, a great many people were being brought to Christ through conversion, baptism and Church membership, the more I investigated the ways in which it had happened, the less I seemed to have to do with it. God works in a mysterious way. I have talked with scores of people who have come to the Christian faith from Hindu or Muslim or Marxist or secular humanist background, and I am always impressed by the fact that the conversion of any person to Christ is a mysterious thing, in which there are many, many different elements, but the strategy is always in the hands of the Holy Spirit. The Holy Spirit Himself, and He alone, is the agent of conversion.

Thirdly, there is the concept of the Church in purely functional terms. I constantly hear people talking about 'Kingdom issues' versus 'Church issues'. 'Forget about the Church, all this ecclesiastical stuff which has nothing to do with God's will. On the last day, when the sheep and the goats are finally separated, they are all irrelevant questions. The important things are Kingdom issues: justice, peace, liberation.' This has a certain element of truth in it. But if it's taken by itself, then the Church just becomes a crusader for liberation which is a very different thing. The Church cannot fulfil the Kingdom purpose that is entrusted to it, — and certainly the Kingdom is the horizon for all our thinking: that God reigns and that the Church is sent into the world a sign of the Kingdom — if it sees its role in merely functional terms. The Church is sign, instrument and foretaste of God's reign for that 'place', that segment of the total fabric of humanity, for which it is responsible — a sign, instrument and foretaste for *that* place with its particular character.

I start with 'foretaste': the great New Testament word *arrabon*, which is such a wonderful word if you think about it. I was once making an elaborate explanation of this word *arrabon* in a class in the Selly Oak colleges and explaining how scholars used to be puzzled by it because it is not a classical Greek word. And then they dug up a lot of parchments in the sands of Egypt and found that they were shopkeepers' accounts and that *arrabon* was just the word that the shopkeepers all used for cash on deposit, a pledge for a bill that you would pay at the end. And an Egyptian student in the class got up and said, 'Well, we still use the same word in Cairo'. Apparently the Arabic word *arbon* is still an operative word. If you want to buy a suit in Cairo you dicker about the cloth and about the style and all that, but before the tailor will start making it he will ask you to put down some cash which is spendable cash, it's not just an IOU. He can go and have a drink with it. The point of that cash, *arbon*, is that it is a pledge that the full bill is going to be paid. And that's the word that St Paul uses over and over again for the Holy Spirit.

If one might use an analogy nearer to home, think of one of those very posh dinner parties where you are kept standing for ages and ages and wonder whether there's ever going to be anything to eat. Then a trolley is brought on and there is a tinkle of glasses, and you are not only extremely glad to get a drink because you're getting very thirsty, but, what is much more important, that trolley is a sign that something is cooking in the kitchen. Now, the Holy Spirit is the *aperitif* for the messianic banquet. It is something which you enjoy now and that is the great thing in the charismatic movement. You enjoy it. There is something really to enjoy and celebrate now. It is not just an IOU, a promissory note. But the whole point of it is that it is a foretaste, that it assures you of a greater reality still to come. And in that sense the Church is a foretaste of the Kingdom.

Here I think the Orthodox have something to teach us. The Orthodox often criticize us in the Western Church for a too functional view of the Church, and I think they are right. The Orthodox have always stressed the point that the Church is first of all a communion in the Holy Spirit in the life of the triune God, so that you must define the Church in ontological terms and not just in functional terms. The Church is defined by what it is. It is already a sharing in the life of God. I felt that tremendously on the occasions when I participated in Orthodox worship in Moscow, where the Church, in functional terms, is almost powerless. It is not allowed to do anything. It's not allowed to preach; it's not allowed to do social work, or to publish anything. But the Church continues to draw converts, and it's just because when you step out of a Moscow street into an Orthodox Church and find yourself in the middle of the Orthodox liturgy, you know that you have stepped out from under one jurisdiction into another jurisdiction. There is another reality there, which just by being what it is challenges the world outside and draws us, because we are made for God and our hearts are restless until they rest in Him. The first thing therefore, is that the Church is a foretaste, and that means it will be different from the world. If it isn't, it's no good. Don't let us be afraid of the fact that the Church is different from the world, that the reality which we celebrate, which we share, which we rejoice in in our worship is a reality which the world treats as an illusion. We must not evade that, or try to slide over it or make it seem less sharp.

But in so far as it is a foretaste, it can also be an instrument. It can be an instrument through which God's will for justice and peace and freedom is done in the world. That takes the Church out into the secular world with whatever is relevant to the real needs of that secular world. If that is not happening, how is the world going to know that the reality we talk about is true? I have recently been very much struck by the fact that if you look at what is often called the mission charge in Matthew Chapter 10, it begins by saying nothing about preaching at all; it simply says that Jesus chose these disciples, and gave them authority over unclean spirits to cast them out and to heal every disease and every infirmity. Then the names of the twelve disciples. And then he goes on to say, 'As you go, preach. And say the Kingdom of God is at hand'. If you look at it that way you can see that the preaching is the explanation of what is happening. If there is nothing happening, there is nothing to explain. But the preaching is a necessary explanation. Other people were healers. Other people cast out devils in the time of Jesus. But if you asked why are devils being cast out, why are people being healed, the answer is that the reign of God is upon you. The preaching explains the happenings.

I used to think about this often in my first charge. I was in a very sacred Hindu city. It is a place which has almost less Western influence than any other city in India, the ancient capital of the Pallava Empire, with a thousand temples and hundreds of thousands of pilgrims who come there every year. And I used to do a lot of street preaching. And I often used to think to myself, 'Now does this do any good? Is this just words?' And I used to reflect that it was because the people there know that we who are standing up and preaching like that are also healing their sick in the hospital, and are also teaching their boys and girls in the schools, and are also helping their village people to do something about their desperate poverty, and are also involved in attempts to make a more just society; it is because they know that, that the words will have some meaning. In other words, that the words without the deeds lack authority! The deeds without the words are dumb, they lack meaning. The two go together. And the Church, in so far as it is a foretaste of the reign of God, can also be an instrument of the reign of God, an instrument by which its justice is done. Not the only instrument of course. God has other instruments — the State is an instrument for God doing justice in the world. I think we have too much neglected this, that God has other instruments for the doing of His will in the world. But it is only the Church which can be the foretaste, the *arrabon* of the Kingdom.

Thirdly, a sign. The point of a sign is that it points to something that is not yet visible. If you want to go to Winson Green you don't put a sign up in Winson Green; you have a sign in Handsworth or Edgbaston or something, which says 'Winson Green'. The point of a sign is that it points to something which is real but not yet visible — which is not visible, not because it does not exist, but because it is over the horizon. Now the Church is a sign of the Kingdom, in so far as it is a foretaste. The Church is a sign of the Kingdom, pointing people to a reality which is beyond what we can see. And the necessary 'other-worldliness' of the Church seems to me to be something that has to be absolutely held on to. We do not compete with all the other agencies in the world that are offering solutions to human problems here and now. We are not offering utopian illusions. We are pointing people to a reality which lies beyond history, beyond death. But we are erecting in this world, here and now, signs — credible signs — that make it possible for people to believe that that is the great reality and, therefore, to join us in going that way.

In all this I've been presupposing the parish model, and I believe that the parish model is the right one. But I recognize the power of the associational model, particularly in its contemporary form. I have recently come to realize how much the 'denomination' has become the model by which we think of the Church, and yet how recent a thing the denomination is. We all tend to think of the Churches as various denominations. And yet the sociologists of religion point out that a denomination is something quite new in church history. It is not a schism, it is not a sect, it doesn't regard itself as the true Church in contrast to the false churches. It is one optional form for the Church, which is in a sense invisible. We cannot apply to the denomination the language that Paul applies to the Church in Corinth, which is the Church of God, full stop. These people in Corinth, sinners as they are, *are* the Church of God, not an expression of it or a version of it. My impression is that through the enormous power of the American model, which tends to dominate the rest of the world, all our Churches are being drawn into this denominational pattern. And my fear is that one of the results of Vatican II might be that the Roman Catholic Church allows itself to be drawn into that model, too.

What the sociologists of religion have pointed out to us is that the denomination is precisely that visible form which the Church takes when a secularized society privatizes religion. The most striking fact about our culture is that we have a dichotomy between the private and the public worlds, a dichotomy which does not exist in pre-modern society. We have a private world of what we call values, where everyone is free to choose his or her own values. We do not say about these that they are true or false. We glory in our pluralism. We say that in the realm of values (and religious beliefs are included in that realm), everyone must be free to have his or her own faith. Pluralism reigns. We also have a public world of what we call facts, where pluralism does not reign, where things are either true or false; and religion does not belong to that field. It does not belong to the public world. Now the denomination is the visible form that the Church takes in a society which has accepted the secularization of public life and the privatization of religion, so that the variety of denominations corresponds, if you like, to the variety of brands available on the shelves of the supermarket. Everyone is free to take his choice.

The denomination, either singly or together, cannot be the bearer of the challenge of the Gospel to our society, because it is itself the outward and visible form of an inward and spiritual surrender to the ideology of that society. And, therefore, if we are to recover the sense that the local church *is* the Holy Catholic Church for that bit of the world in which God has set it (and that is the parish principle) then we have to challenge this whole accept-ance of the denominational principle as being the normal form in which Church life is expressed. I find this both a necessary and a frightening thought. I cannot avoid it if I try to be faithful to the scriptures, but I find it terribly challenging.

I have referred earlier to my own personal situation. I am the minister of a very small URC congregation in Winson Green. How do I try to carry out these ideas there? We have the parish church; we have a Pentecostal church; we have another URC church; we have a black church called the Church of the First-born; and we, without formally being a Local Ecumenical Project (because I don't think our higher authorities would allow it), simply act together as clergy. We meet together constantly. We pray together constantly. We plan together constantly. We try to ask what, in spite of our divisions, our unity in Christ has to mean for the life of this community in Winson Green.

It seems to me that the development of that kind of local accepting of one another, in spite of our divisions and our misunderstandings, is the Catholic Church in that place seeking to erect the sign of the Kingdom for that place. These two things are mutually involved. I do not think we shall recover the true form of the parish until we recover a truly missionary approach to our culture. I do not think we shall achieve a truly missionary encounter with our culture without recovering the true form of the parish. These two tasks are reciprocally related to each other, and we have to work together on them both.

4

A Cross-Bench View of Associational Religion

David Martin

Sociology cannot answer evaluative questions about the social role of the Church; it can however clarify thinking by elucidating unacknowledged presuppositions which may be shaping current attitudes and behaviour. Study of large-scale and long-term patterns in religious behaviour offers nothing to substantiate theories about the practice of religion which are based either on Scriptural norms, attitudes to liturgy, or ecumenism. The experience of the British Churches over the past two centuries, particularly the shift towards 'associational' church life, is characteristic of North America and northern Europe generally. Where denominations actively compete for members, as in North America, associational churches also have significant community functions. 'State monopoly' churches, a feature of Scandinavia, are characterized by tiny associational churches coupled with a widespread but crumbling 'folk' religiosity. Devising 'communitarian' forms is unlikely to affect this general pattern. But the idea of the parish and the church as a focus of meaning and continuity may still be worth believing in.

Insofar as the theme of the seminar implies an ethical evaluation of the parish church, I am not certain that as a sociologist I can be of much help. In any case, sociologists have not done a great deal of work on the parish. Sociologists are often asked in at this curious axis between description and evaluation, and one has constantly to say that, as a sociologist, one has no way of making evaluative comments. That is not to say, of course, that sociologists never abandon their role, but one does want to distinguish very clearly between description and evaluation.

What sociologists can do, even in situations about which they know rather little, *e.g.* the parish, is to be brutally frank about what they think the presuppositions are which underpin thinking in this area. They can look at those presuppositions and maybe say something about them, and they can also set out the social context insofar as it limits choices and constrains the outcome of choices. They can say, 'Well, if you do so and so, there are only a limited range of choices available'; or, 'You may do so and so, but you are constrained and the outcomes can only be of this and this kind'. And that may be quite a useful function. Reading the paper prepared by the Core Group, and Bishop Newbigin's paper, there appears to be a kind of 'sub-text'. Let me try to expound it. There appear to be four main themes.

First, that ever since the break-up of an organic society, which I suppose one would put at around 1760 and 1840, churches have become increasingly 'denominational', increasingly 'congregational', and increasingly inclined to serve particular status groups rather more than others. They have been increasingly drawing people together within limits which are set by social affinity rather than by local community. I suppose that is the crucial notion of the associational kind, social affinity rather than local community. And the residual pull of locality comes down in considerable measure to the limit which is set by distance; people do not really want to go all that far to church.

Now in that situation, where the status differences have been sharp, they have combined with theological differences to fragment the Church into rival denominations: that is to say, we have a basically splintered and fragmented situation. The Church is a combination of social distance and theological difference, and the two are constantly reinforcing each other. And different denominations compete by offering marginally differentiated products on the market. But whatever they offer, it is all within the basic associational format, with one major exception, and that is where the Church (reverting to that term) happens to provide the binding elements in a minority ethnic group. The most obvious case in Britain is where the Roman Catholic Church has provided the binding element for say, Polish migrants or Irish migrants, or, say, in America where Norwegian Lutherans settled in a particular area and so you have a Norwegian Lutheran community Church.

Secondly, status groups to which the churches or denominations have appealed have been higher rather than lower. The Church is most successful in middle-class areas, where it accepts a variety of styles, catering for different status groups. Not only do different churches devise particular, marginally differentiated products, but inside themselves they devise a different product according to different status groups. In that sort of middle-class area there is also a segmenting of roles, whereby the church-going element in a person's life is just one among many others. Of course, the Church may help to energize a person's commitments, but those are mostly worked out outside the Church itself.

If one were to turn away from the suburbs to the Church in the inner city, even there it appeals to those who are relatively better off, so that within any given grouping it is the relatively better off who are attracted to the Church. And in the inner city, as you know, the Church is anyway not an active focus of community, at least so far as worship goes.

Thirdly, this situation of ineffectiveness in the city and of privatization in the suburbs is labelled 'associational'. The counter to it is the 'parish', which I think may be a code-word for some kind of 'communitarian' notion, even perhaps a 'communitarian nostalgia'.

Fourthly, this challenge in the name of 'the parish' is legitimated by the kind of appeal to Scripture which was made by Bishop Newbigin. I have to say that I find this legitimation tenuous. It is highly inspirational and quite exciting, but I do not

see that there is much connection between what the Bible had to
say about the Church in Corinth, and what goes on in Surbiton or in
Consett, County Durham. What Bishop Newbigin seemed to be
saying was that the Church which is at Surbiton should be 'for'
Surbiton, and that word 'for' seems to have a lot of meanings in it
which I wasn't very certain about. All I could see was that it meant
that the Church in Surbiton should be interested in Surbiton. And
my response to that was that I hoped it was interested in Surbiton
but I didn't have very optimistic expectations about how far organic
Christian communitarianism was likely to get in Surbiton, or in
Consett, County Durham, for that matter. So I was a bit sceptical
about what really lay behind Bishop Newbigin's eloquent words.

Let me respond to that sub-text by placing it in a sociological
context. The associational model is characteristic of developed
Europe and North America. It is especially characteristic of the
North European 'Protestant' plain (*i.e.* Birmingham to Helsinki).
There is an inclination on the part of English clergy to feel that
there is a specifically Anglican failure. But there just isn't, there is a
uniform failure. From Birmingham to Helsinki there is the same
situation.

That situation is most obvious where there are state monopoly
churches, as in Scandinavia. It is least obvious in North America
where there are very numerous competing denominations. They
are certainly associational, but they have also developed extensive
community functions. I am enormously impressed when I go to
some Lutheran church on the margin of some city that has only
been put up within ten years, and it is absolutely riddled with
community functions. It is really doing an extraordinary business in
putting out tentacles into the wider community.

What one sees in Scandinavia is not this lively, competing,
fragmented, associational form characteristic of North America,
but an already ecumenical situation. That is, there is a monopoly
Church in Scandinavia which is utterly ecumenical, apart from
Pentecostals and a few migrants. The competition is *very* limited.
There is a tiny associational Church above an ex-localized base,
coupled with a vast area of apathetic 'folk' adherence in process of
erosion.

England is to my mind poised between Scandinavia and North America but leaning quite sharply in the Scandinavian direction. We, like Berlin and Amsterdam, are part of the lower tentacles of the Scandinavian icecap.

That decides the broader sociological context. When one comes down to the inner-city situation, it seems to me to be simply the most dramatic consequence of certain very general processes. They are very usefully summarized in a book by Dr Hugh McLeod of Birmingham University, called *Religion and the Working Class in Nineteenth Century Britain.*[1] It is very neat and clear, and uncontaminated by personal viewpoints. What he says is that between 1880 and 1930, first the rich and powerful became less and less interested in religion, so certain supports from there began to disappear. Secondly, that the labour movement built up an a-religious sub-culture (and I would stress the a-religious rather than the anti-religious; if you compared Germany and Scandinavia with England there was a much stronger anti-religious element in Germany and Scandinavia as compared with the a-religious element that one finds in Britain). Thirdly, that paternalist local firms with links with local church or chapel were absorbed into large combines.[2] Fourthly, that the expanding services of local and central government and of the leisure industry marginalized the extensive services which were offered by the churches. Let me quote McLeod here: '. . . It was not until with the radio and the beginnings of the cinema craze in the 1920s that the churches' functions as providers of cheap amusement were essentially superseded.'

Whatever may have been the case in some other parts of Europe, the construction of ideological alternatives to Christianity in some kind of socialist sub-culture was much less important in England than the car, the garden, a snooze over the *News of the World*, and just that vague sense of 'us and them'. I would add that the Church's input into education through its colleges has become eroded. Quite a lot of diffused Christianity was mediated through female primary-school teachers, and that particular channel is being silted up.

Let me stress that this Protestant North European situation is very general. There are only two alternatives that I can see. There is the American pattern, which most of us know about, one where practically half the society is in church anyway on a given Sunday. The other alternative is the Southern European pattern of rabid clericalism and equally rabid anti-clericalism. That pattern was dominant from 1790 to 1960 in Catholic countries. And as the collision of clerical and anti-clerical dies away, what tends to take its place is a kind of consumerist apathy such as one sees occurring very rapidly in Spain over the last ten years, and which has occurred equally rapidly but over a longer period in the Church of France. (Whenever we are talking about comparisons, as Mr Clifford Longley in *The Times* is constantly inviting us to make comparisons between the Church of England and the Roman Catholic Church in this country, the proper comparison is with the Church of France, and the Church of France has experienced something almost identical with what the Church of England has experienced.)

Now if this is the situation, it is important that the Church does not think that certain kinds of *ad hoc* contingent strategies are somehow going to provide the golden key which will transform everything.

The situation is not going to be changed by particular alterations in styles of communication, certainly not in the field of liturgy. Indeed, so far as the Roman Catholic Church is concerned, one can say without much fear of contradiction that over the whole of the Roman Catholic Church in the developed world, what has happened since 1962 has been quite sharp declines: in other words, Vatican II initiated a whole series of initial excitements, and then sharp declines. Now, as a sociologist, I am definitely not going to go around saying, 'get rid of the Latin Mass and you end up with 35 per cent less attendance, or whatever': one cannot make that kind of causal link. One *can* say that a whole set of assumptions about the relationship of the Church to culture, particularly Protestant or proto-Protestant notions about how communities are held together, seeped into the Roman Catholic Church, and destroyed some of the strong bonds which it had built up between 1860 and 1960. Now I happen not to approve of those bonds. Let me make it perfectly clear, I do not approve of 'fortress

catholicism', or 'ghetto catholicism', post-Vatican I, which was
built up as a barrier to the modern world and in particular as a
counterblast to liberalism. What I do believe, as a sociologist, is
that the liberalizing notions that got into the Catholic Church
after 1960, did a great deal of organizational damage, dramati-
cally so in certain places like Holland and in America. You may
say they got closer to the theological truth *and* lost people. That
is the kind of schizophrenic situation in which I as a sociologist
find myself. What I am saying is that one cannot suppose that by
producing a new book of liturgy or a new style of communication
or whatever, one somehow is going to transform the overall
situation.

Another supposition which I think is wrong is that 'ecumenism'
will do something about it. Looking over the general situation, I
think that ecumenism is associated with weakness and competition is associated with strength. That does not mean that by
immediately having a series of rapid schisms one can restore the
health of Christianity in England and Scandinavia. It is only to say
that in those situations which we see to be competitive, it looks as
if the Church is at least healthy in organizational terms. Those
situations where there is the most complete monopoly, as in
Scandinavia, are deadliest in organizational terms. There is a kind
of folk supposition that because Christianity has become fragmented, it has lost its power to affect the populations. I do not
believe that to be true. I know of course that from time to time
when one talks to people they may say, 'Oh!, look at the Church's
divisions', and it may be in the mission field that there are all
kinds of complications arising from European-based schism. But in
general I do not believe that ecumenism will make much
difference.

Another supposition that might be around, and I am not sure
how far it is around, is that if the lack of resources were got rid of,
then much more could be done. I do not know how much truth
there is generally in this, but I went to Finland twice in the
summer, and there is a Church with the most incredible resources.
There is no problem at all about the resources. I went to the kinds
of country retreat places where young people go for confirmation.

(Incidentally, 90 per cent of young people are confirmed in Finland.) These were most beautifully set up with all the educational resources you can imagine, but the organizational health of the Finnish Church in terms of weekly attendance runs in the inner city at between half and one per cent, and for the country overall at four per cent. The figures for state churches all over this area are almost identical. I am almost horrified as a sociologist at the degree to which these things repeat themselves. One is in a discipline where one often talks about inability to make generalizations, but the startling similarity and the generality of these things is what strikes one in this instance.

Thus it is not a matter of resources, though no doubt some resources would not do any harm. Nor is it a lack of intellectual modernity. Of course different intellectual styles are devised by the different constituencies. What goes on in Emmanuel College Chapel and what goes on in other places will clearly differ quite considerably, but I do not believe that some kind of liberalized up-dating of the Church's doctrine or understanding will make the faintest bit of difference. My feeling is that, for example, with regard to process theology, congregations do not want it and the priests that preach it do not understand it, because it actually requires an awful lot of work if you are going to preach that kind of thing without falling over into really quite complicated theological holes. So *not* some kind of liberalization. And yet people like David Jenkins do actually think that part of the trouble is not being up-to-the-minute in terms of doctrinal advance or change.

Nor does the situation have a great deal to do with how much the Church is involved in making left-liberal proclamations to society at large. It may well be that part of the way the Church speaks to this society is through the media. It may be that it has now acquired a kind of 'media pulpit', through which it engages in different kinds of social critique. But I do not believe that that makes any difference either. I see no association between the liveliness of Christianity and the extent to which such comments are made by the Church.

Finally, I don't think that devising 'communitarian' forms as distinct from 'associational' ones really cuts into the problem. I hope that does not sound too negative, because I actually favour the parish and would like to say why. Although there are so many social trends moving against 'the parish', it seems to me to have certain strengths and virtues. Many of the networks of charity, of voluntary work and of the arts, especially music, link up with the social network of the parish. I recognize that this is not so in certain areas where the Church's work has particularly broken down. Then, there is a latent 'folk' religion which, while intermittent in its practice, does have some kind of focus in the parish church, notably through the rites of passage. I think, incidentally, that any attempt to be sectarian in respect of rites of passage is a big mistake. To insist on particular kinds of commitment on the part of parents may have some slight effect in drumming up a certain amount of commitment, but overall its effect is negative.

I would also say that the parish church offers some kind of focus of meaning which is embodied architecturally. I think that it was Bruce Reed who commented that it was often the only non-utilitarian building in certain areas. It is *there*; it would be a great shame if it were not there, and not understood to be the parish church. People are still in some ways *located*; whatever social and geographical mobility does to them, many people retain a sense of place, a sense of origin, a sense of continuity. For that matter, recent research indicates that social and geographical mobility is not so peculiar to our own time as we think it is; goes back several hundred years. So it is in 'place' that continuities are sought and still maintained.

5

The Ideological Corruption of a National Church

Clifford Longley

A non-Anglican can discern features of the life of the Church of England which are not apparent to Anglicans: its confusion between the Church as institution and the Church as bricks and mortar; its uncritical acceptance of Establishment and the link with royalty and Parliament; its clericalism. These are all aspects of a potentially corrupting ideological captivity of the Church. It blinds Anglican to other models of church life than the parish church model, notably basic communities, and distracts the Church from its essential task, which is to help people grow as spiritual beings.

Somebody once asked me in connection with my Chapel activity (the branch organization of journalists) whether the Church came into it. I scratched my head a bit: it's true we have held a couple of meetings in the crypt of St George's in the East. I suppose in that way the Anglican Church has provided us with some warm accommodation, for which of course we are grateful (though I would add that we had to pay for it). In other respects it is not possible to answer the question, except in a rather more subtle way. Of course the Church comes into my job. I am involved in it, and I am one of those Christians who cannot make a separation between the person I am, wearing one hat, and the person I am, wearing another. I cannot help but recognize that to some extent people will be measuring the Church by how I behave in those circumstances. If I behave in a way that is cynical and dishonest, this will do enormous damage to the reputation of the Church, because there is a sense in which we are all representatives, whether we are lay or clerical. I don't find that a very comfortable feeling, because I have to recognize that a lot of damage can be caused by inadvertent, or careless, or unscrupulous behaviour if I was tempted to do that. So the Church does come into it, and indeed it comes into it in a more profound way, the Church being people not buildings. Which leads me to my main topic.

It's important to recognize that the Church of England has tended to make an identification between the Church as institution and community, with the church, the building. This is one of a number of things that someone like me, who is not an Anglican, sees as quite distinctive about Anglicanism, which those who are Anglicans may take for granted as an unexamined assumption. I have the advantage of not being within that Anglican culture, though I am familiar with it; and occasionally I stub my toe on things like that and say to myself, 'Hang on a sec, perhaps that ought not to be so, or perhaps it isn't so'. So the observation that the Church is people not buildings, though it might sound like a platitude, is an insight into my own thinking on the question, 'Do we need the Parish church?', because I am sure that question is often read as, 'Do we need the building, do we need the bricks and mortar?'

Anglicans tend very strongly to relate to a particular pile of bricks and mortar. They use the word 'church' without recognizing that in fact they are referring to two different kinds of concept. 'Church' as building and 'Church' as institution somehow get muddled together into this one single Church, so the feeling, the impression, the smell, *is* the structure. The sensation of being 'in church' is not just a sensation of being in the presence of the holy, but the sensation of being surrounded by a particular piece of architecture.

I have to record that on reading through the Core Group's discussion paper I did find it *very* Anglican. There was a curious flavour to it which would make it quite impossible for that paper to have been produced by any other denomination: it is riddled with unexamined assumptions which are quite distinctively Anglican. It makes me nervous to think that you have gone quite a long way into the seminar process without ever having your attention drawn to these unexamined assumptions.

In particular, I was very uneasy at the psychological analysis contained in the paper. The paper relied so heavily upon projection, that it seemed to me that it had ignored the possibility that there are quite other systematic ways of analysing the things that are being analysed. There seems to me a restrictiveness and a narrowness about the paper, basically because it takes this particular psychological insight as if it said all that needed to be said, whereas in fact the subject can be looked at from a number of different perspectives, and maybe this particular psychological one is not going to take us very far. I feel you have narrowed yourselves down to a particular set of theories about the relationship between the parish church and the community at large, and this may have deprived you of opportunities of looking at it in other ways.

I am going to try to present a slightly different approach. I want to apply the concept of ideology, to talk about the relationship between the parish church looking downwards towards the local community and looking upwards towards the nation. The parish church as part of a wider community has a special significance, in that it is the level at which people's perceptions of themselves as members of the Church and members of a local community are most closely tied together. There is a sense in which if one looks at the institutional life of the Church at a national level you see the wider community of the nation on one hand, and you see the life of the Church structurally on the other: the sort of things you read about in the *Church Times* and occasionally in *The Times*, but very rarely in *The Guardian!* At the parish level there is the closest sense of identity between the Church and the community. We see this in various respects. It is part of the commitment of an Anglican clergyman, and indeed of the core of active lay people he will have around him, that they serve the wider community, they serve the total population contained within the geographical limits of their particular parish rather than a 'sectarian' (a very commonly used Anglican word in this context) group of people who have membership of the electoral roll or are regular church attenders, or whose names are known to the vicar, however one defines the much smaller group. It is a conspicuous part of Anglican ideology to regard oneself as having a responsibility to the total community, and this is very strongly expressed at parish church level, more successfully than at national level. I am by no means the only person who found himself a little surprised on reading *Faith in the City* to see how the Church rather effortlessly appointed itself the conscience of the nation. That self-appointment puts enormous irritation on people who don't see things that way. In other words, when the step is taken from that kind of relationship between Church and parish at grass roots level, to the same kind of identification at national level, it becomes very much more questionable. Nevertheless the parish church, at the basic level of serving the local community's needs, or at least wanting to, is a very distinctive part of the Church of England as a national Church. It is probably the most important part of its character as a national Church, given the hesitation I have about the national Church having some sort of role as the conscience of the nation. In other words, it is much more acceptable to me to think of a comprehensive relationship to the community at the local level, than to think of it at a national level.

There is an ecclesiology innate and implicit in the way the Church of England functions, of which expressions such as 'the

National Church' are an important clue. This ecclesiology, when coupled with Establishment, amounts to an ideology. Let me tell you how I am using the word ideology. It refers not just to ideas, but to a structure of ideas which is largely hidden, while the ideas themselves are familiar. So one has a range of notions which are connected underneath the soil, so to speak, but one is not aware of the connections, only of the notions themselves. I believe there is a very substantial element of ideology in the concept of the Church of England as National Church and as an established Church. It is summed up by such expressions as 'Anglicanism', or that the Church of England is the natural religion of the English. A common assumption is that when somebody decides that they wish to be more religious than they have been in the past, it is the Church of England that they would naturally turn to. There is also an assumption that when the word 'church' is used in ordinary conversation, it is the Church of England which is being referred to. This is true not only of the one-and-a-half million Anglicans who attend church every week, but of the population at large. This perception of an ideological element in the relationship between Church and society can be detected in people who do not go to church at all or have very little interest in the Church. The ideological element in it is important to bring out, because I believe there are grounds for seeing ideology as a danger to religion. For example, when Paul warns about the world it may be ideology he is talking about: the way in which worldly things can corrupt the things of the Spirit.

I suggest that there is an ideological corruption present in the Church of England's ecclesiology because of its association with Establishment and with its role as the National Church. I'm not trying to score partisan points as a Roman Catholic; I would probably be saying a very similar thing about the French Roman Catholic Church if I was sitting in Paris rather than in London. It is in relation to the notion of Establishment and of a National Church that this ideological element comes in. The Elizabethan Settlement was a very important moment in the establishment of this ideology, not just because it was from there that the essential shape of Establishment emerged, but because it was from there that other things emerged with a strong ideological content, such as the concept of nationalism. The Reformation of which the Elizabethan Settlement was a part was a moment when the mediaeval idea of a United States of Europe broke up into nation states. The English experience is a very striking instance of this. At the time of Henry or Elizabeth a kind of drawbridge was pulled up at Calais; from then on the sense of being English was the sense of being stuck against the world. We still have a strong sense as English people that the normal and natural way of being a human being is to be an Englishman. It is very difficult for us to adjust to the notion that the Italians regard the normal and natural way of being a human being as being an Italian. The ideology of nationalism emerged at the same time as the ecclesiology of establishment was being determined and they are closely related. The sense of sovereignty over religion and over moral and cultic belief which was established in the Elizabethan Settlement was an important step in the formation of the ideology of nationalism, and this concept has now been adopted universally and has been reflected in the fragmentation of communities throughout the world. It would have been a quite alien idea to our mediaeval ancestors; they would have found this a very strange thing indeed. They would have been more acutely aware than we are that it contains a very strong ideological element, although of course they wouldn't have had the concept of ideology.

We say that the middle-class, white, middle-aged English experience of being human is the normal way of being human. It is surprisingly the case that that model has, to a certain extent, become normative throughout the world. It is strange that the Japanese expression for the clothes worn by a respectable businessman is 'Savile Row', and throughout the world you will find Japanese businessmen having lunch with Indonesian businessmen in darkest Africa trying to behave like English gentlemen. The concept we tend rather to mock at, of being a human being in England, is in fact accepted throughout the world, though if you put it specifically, it would be denied.

Now, having introduced this emphasis on ideology, I want to talk about some quite specific elements in it. First, the Church of

England puts a really astonishing amount of weight on its relationship with royalty. The Church of England somehow or other seems to have invested royalty with almost divine qualities, and this obsession with royalty seems to have got out of hand. I am not referring here to the popular press's treatment of it, I am talking about the way in which average people feel about the Royal Family, and the Queen in particular. Somehow or other the Church of England has invested that person, who is a human being exactly like us, with qualities which are not exactly like us, with quasi-divine qualities. It is almost as if the Queen is seen as somehow or other to be not quite human. It is an extraordinary fact that something like two-thirds of the British people at some point or another have a dream about the Queen coming to tea. It is amazing how deeply this has gone. It is an extraordinary fact that at a subconscious level we have elevated royalty, and invested royalty with religious qualities, and I believe we cannot talk about the ideology of the Church and its relationship with society in general unless we look at that.

Secondly, there are ideological assumptions, present though totally unexamined, when we think about the relationship between Church and Parliament. In Parliament, as you are well aware, there are mechanisms whereby measures from the Church of England are submitted for a process of approval. They can be defeated, but if they are not defeated then they become law. It is taken for granted that this should be the case, and it is not questioned. It seems to me very strange that there has been so little interest in the Church of England in this relation with the establishment. I believe the reason is that you are in an ideological lock and it is impossible, or at least very hard, for you to do so. I said before that ideology is a danger to the Church as an organization. We have to take seriously the possibility that there is a kind of corruption in this ideological element in the relationship between Church and Society. The Church of England holds together, in spite of having some very strong diverse elements, because of the way it works with the Establishment. If Establishment as an ideology were changed, I cannot see the Church of England going on holding in tension extreme evangelicals and extreme anglo-catholics. They are held in one society because of this matrix called Establishment.

Let me give you an illustration of the relationship between Church and Society at the parish level. Is the Church of England handling to the best advantage the resources it has? I went to Merseyside to talk to local clergy in order to produce a report on how in working class areas lay people, church and clergy, could relate to the parish. There was a contrast between the Church of England and the Roman Catholic Church. The Church of England church in one neighbourhood had one clergyman who had the almost hopeless job, based on a brief he had accepted, of relating to the spiritual needs of some X thousand people, with a congregation of 15 to 20, and no way of relating to the secular life except as a treasurer of a housing association. He suffered profound anguish daily, associated with the kind of achievement he had set himself, and it was clearly impossible to meet the spiritual needs of so many. He experienced failure every day. He had automatically accepted the idea of the parish church.

The next day I went to an identical Roman Catholic parish. There was a different structure, where the priest was not trying to relate to the 8000 who were identified as Roman Catholics. Unlike the Anglican clergyman, who walked around smiling a lot, the Roman Catholic priest had a specific set of tasks to get through from morning to evening and was perfectly capable of doing them and telling himself he had done them. The Anglican was deeply demoralized: the Roman Catholic was not.

The threat to the Anglican system arises partly from the encroachment of secularism, which seems to me to be a necessary accompaniment to the growth of liberal democracy and the way institutions of the state take over from the Church, but also from the shrinking of the Church of England's numerical base in society, which makes it very hard to go on believing that it is still capable of meeting this comprehensive service to the community. It would be better for the Church of England, were it to become more modest in its ambitions, and to recognize that the success of the community was not somehow or other the responsibility of Anglicans, if only they knew how to exercise it, but that out there in the community at large there are identifiable points that the Church can reach and relate to. Just as there is within any total

community an invisible structure of Roman Catholic family networks, so there is an identical structure of Anglican networks. It
seems to me that the Church of England would be doing itself a
very great favour were it to concentrate a bit more on those
points within the network, and a bit less on this hopeless black
hole, in trying to meet the needs of the total community. This is
usually shot down with the word 'sectarian'. I find that an
ideological blocking which we have to find some way round. The
word 'sectarian' should be dropped from the vocabulary, because
it stops what might well be a fruitful way of thinking about the
problems of the Church relating to the community at the parish
level. In fact, if an Anglican clergyman, like my friend on
Merseyside, had a structured day, it would give him a precise
sense of what he had to achieve from morning to evening, and
the possibility of going to bed saying, 'Well I have done today
what was expected of me'. It would bring the problems down to a
manageable level and they could be broken up and analysed.

There are further influences leading to obvious breakdown.
Several of them are things one would want to welcome, such as
ecumenism. The Church of England is going to find an increasing strain on its comprehensiveness by such activities as ARCIC.
The Covenant for unity a few years ago was a strain in the other
direction, and it was widely said then that the Church of
England would probably not come out in one piece if the Covenant went through. Evidence is now beginning to emerge that it
is not easy to see how the Church of England can come through
in one piece if ARCIC goes through. No doubt you are aware of
the growing grumblings from the extreme evangelical element in
the Church of England that the 39 Articles and the Protestant
Reformation heritage are all at risk under the ARCIC process. It
is a sign of the times that not only has the Church Society
threatened to break away, but also that the Church Union at the
other end has been talking in the same language. You will
remember the Bishop of London's reference to the possibility of a
'continuing Church' last year. These problems, although they
seem to be doctrinal and theological, are very relevant to the
question whether you can go on talking about the Church

having a service to the total community. There may be tensions within the Church which are going to change its nature, regardless of how you answer this question of the parish church and the total community.

There are other alternative models to the Anglican parish church, which do not have the same ideological content. The Church of England has become rather interested of late in notions associated with the theology of liberation, such as 'Basic Communities'. The Tiller Report, for example, which clearly some important influences in the Church are anxious to promote, uses the concept of basic communities taken from the theology of liberation, involving a moving away from the notion of the parish church towards more tightly knit and much more self-conscious communities, which are no longer thought to be identical to the population covered by the parish but are much more identifiably the Church in that neighbourhood. The basic community idea seems to me a very important thing to examine, because it has the advantage of being free of the ideological dangers of the parish system we have at the moment.

I want to end by taking the basic community idea a little further. An important element in what the Church does at the grass roots level is better discharged by something like a basic community than by the parish church. For all that is said in the discussion document about the healthy form of the parish church, there are a lot of distractions present at the parish church level which would not be present at the basic community level, so the basic community would be clearer about what it was trying to do.

In the parish church it is very easy for religion to become a kind of hobby, another way of creating a small circle of friends whom you can relate to, another way of doing interesting things, another way of filling time. There are enormous numbers of such things in society, of which the Church is only one more, and not necessarily a very distinctive one. I am well aware, having come back into the NUJ scene having been absent for about twelve years, of the way that for many people the NUJ is a hobby. They put just the kind of energy into running that organization that I see put into running a parish church. It is precisely the same experience, it provides the same kind of social need, the same sense of purpose, which I believe is, sadly, a profoundly mistaken sense of purpose. People are seeking society, friendship, association, relationship, company. It does not really matter where it occurs, it is good that it should occur, but it is wrong to label it specifically or narrowly 'church'. We meet our needs for social contact in a thousand ways, and it is quite wrong and quite mistaken of the Church to think that it has some kind of corner in doing that. There is a considerable danger in the existing parish church structure operating as a focus for 'hobby' church-manship. I don't wish to knock it, I just don't wish to see the Church distracted by providing that kind of function in society.

What is inseparable from the purpose of the Church, something for which gardening societies, NUJ, or anything else cannot be a substitute, is that it is a focus, a kind of school, where one may hope to grow and change oneself by making use of the potential for spiritual development which comes from pursuing the Christian life. That is what the parish church fundamentally ought to be doing. If it cannot do it, and I strongly suspect it cannot, we need to turn to such things as basic communities to see if they can. Religion is not something which you either do or don't do, it is something you do more of, you grow into. I believe that religion is essentially concerned with the profound formation of personality, and those who are serious about their commitment to the religious life must allow themselves sufficient exposure to it to let this profound formation of personality occur. That cannot be done if one is using the Church as some kind of hobby. It cannot be done under existing parish structures, where the only people who are really expected to take that kind of thing seriously are the clergy, while the laity are allowed to tag along more or less perpetually on the bottom rung of the ladder. Everybody accepts that they are essentially second class Christians, and the only people who are expected to pray daily or say the office daily, or who are expected to expose themselves to the possibility of the process of spiritual formation, are the clergy, not the laity.

So we have here encountered yet another kind of ideology, the ideology of clericalism. I don't propose to analyse it for you: I just leave it with you.

6

Making God Findable

Helen Oppenheimer

Society needs the Church because the Christian faith is true. The associational model of the Church fails to commend the Christian faith, by equating it with joining a religious group. The demand for commitment suggests that God puts conditions on His grace. But those who practise their religion are to be seen not as morally superior to, but as representing, all the others. The parish church in principle symbolizes the availability of God and puts people in touch with him particularly through the sacraments. The Church is the host, receiving, listening and confronting with a distinctive presence.

Even if society still thinks it needs the parish church, the only reason for encouraging this belief is that the Christian faith is true. We must not acquiesce in basing needs on a lie. If Christianity were just an attractive fiction like Father Christmas, people really ought to learn to live without it. We mustn't say, 'Come to us for consolation. Never mind the dogmas. Support the parish church and we will christen your children, bless your marriages and bury your dead'. Mainly we must be saying: 'There is God.' But out in the world, the question is, Why do we believe in God anyway? One of the great changes of our time is that the onus is now on us to say why, as opposed to the onus being on other people to say why not.

For our present purpose we may affirm, 'there is God' as our basis and go on to ask: granted this, that God is, what are we to say about what God is like, and what are we really conveying not only by our words but by our deeds and omissions? We can be more specific: granted that society does indeed need the Christian faith because the Christian faith is the truth, does it need the Christian faith in the form of the parish church, or does it need to be challenged by forms of 'church' which are less to be taken for granted?

Having put the question in this way, I myself run into three difficulties. The first difficulty is that I am supposed to be some sort of moral theologian. Doesn't this question turn itself either into one about the strategy and tactics of mission, what will or won't work, or into a sociological question about what our society at the present time is like? At least it *looks* as if it had a rather obvious sociological answer. On ordinary Sundays society shows very little sign of needing a parish church; but society still has needs (which the parish church is filling but increasingly reluctantly) for acknowledging an extra dimension to human life and especially at its great milestones. Society, whatever that exactly is, wants to celebrate births and marriages, to mourn and give thanks for the dead, to cheer itself up in the middle of winter, to link itself somehow to the world of nature and the fruitfulness of the earth, and to mark its solemn national occasions. The shorthand for this at the moment is 'folk religion'. 'Folk religion' needs rites of passage, and so it does. Whether we say this in a dismissive or a pleading or even a triumphant voice is a matter of theology, of what we believe about God. What I hope to do is take, as given, what common sense and the sociologists are able to tell me about how our society is, and try to say something about how Christian theology can be applied to this.

My second difficulty is that what I am taking as given is hardly typical. I live in Jersey where the parish structure is very much alive both in theory and in practice. The twelve historic parishes are also the units of local government. The parish hall is a centre for both civic and church occasions. Voters are called 'parishioners.' The parish really matters. We don't have to work up enthusiasm for it; and the church is very much part of this. We are a rural parish. The harvest festival means a lot to us perfectly naturally, and indeed theother rural festivals (Plough Sunday, Rogation, Lammas). When it comes to the harvest festival the church is full of local produce, not tins of pineapple. When we pray for our Constable, the civil officer of the parish, and our Deputy, they are people we know and we can approach. So church and state go along together and we are conscious of being a community, because the whole thing is on a human scale.

In the present context all this is a difficulty because am I thereby hopelessly blinkered? Has everything moved on in ways I haven't noticed? I think of Psalm 16: 'The lot is fallen unto me in a fair ground'. Am I merely encouraging a fiction and living in the past? If I were to take the line, 'Up with the parish: look at Jersey and how well we do things there', I should run the risk of unrealistic irrelevance. That is why I like the Core Group's paper, because from the English context, not necessarily so favourable, it still offers very good reasons for approving the 'parish model'. Of course the parish church has its fiction that this is a Christian country; but the associational church also has its subtler and more dangerous fiction, that 'repent and believe the Gospel' is exactly the same thing as 'be committed, join a church'. A certain sort of belonging is the will of God for all our contemporaries, and must therefore be a live option for everybody. And yet, don't we know people who would be diminished, not fulfilled, humanly speaking, if they took up that way of belonging, our way of doing things? Can't the Holy Spirit appreciate their independence perhaps more, not less, than we can, and is there no room in the Kingdom for this sort of diversity of vocation? I believe the parish church, with its fiction that it is ministering to everyone, is a less misleading model than the associational church with its fiction that we can all be expected to be joiners of societies.

I get to my third difficulty. Does this paper fit my preconceptions *too* well? So let me say what I warmed to so much, and then acknowledge the real theological difficulties in my position and so try to bring the argument to a head. I especially warmed to the idea of making everyone welcome and not being ungracious to 'folk religion' and fringe religion. Some years ago, travelling in Turkey, my husband and I went to the shrine and tomb of Mevlana who founded the whirling dervishes, at Konya, and written up near his tomb, translated into English, there was a verse which I much warmed to. It read something like this (I wrote it down from memory, but I think I have got it right):

Come, come, whoever or whatever you may be, come.
Infidel, heathen, fireworshipper, idolater, come.
Though you have broken your penitence a hundred times,
Ours is not the portal of despair and misery, come.

It seemed to me, can't we as Christians do as well as this? For Christians, the ground of saying this kind of thing is that Christ died for all. We seem shy of being so welcoming. We make conditions. I want to argue now that in so doing we are precisely Pharisaical, by which I don't mean proud. I don't mean lacking in compassion, I mean making void the word of God by our tradition. The whole point about the Pharisees, of course, is that they had an excellent tradition of loyal devotion to the service of God, just as we have. (The Pharisees have had a bad press. I expect you all know the story of the teacher who told her class the story of the Pharisee and the Publican, and then said, 'Now, children, we must thank God that we are just ordinary people, not like the nasty Pharisee'.)

This is not an argument about how to be good, but an argument about the nature of God; and it is an argument in which the answer is not obvious. It is time now to try to be fair to the reasons why many people want to go back to the Pharisaical virtues, to keep God's laws, and withdraw themselves from the worldly accommodations of 'folk religion'; why they want to belong to a church that makes real demands on them, a church that they cannot take for granted. To what kinds of God are we witnessing? Many people feel that the parish church today, nearly empty on ordinary Sundays and full for human special occasions, witnesses to a God we can comfortably forget most of the time, a soft God who will never be angry with us, an almost mechanical God who will doggedly keep on doing his job, a sort of extra special government official or social worker, at worst the taxman, at best Father Christmas making seasonal appearances in a traditional outfit, encouraging us to specify what we want to make us happy; or maybe a kind shoulder to weep on when things go wrong. None of that, we know perfectly well, is the Christian faith. Isn't the real thing well summed up at the beginning of Mark's Gospel, 'The time is fulfilled and the Kingdom of God is at hand; repent and believe the Gospel'? Doesn't that perhaps point straight to the associational church?

If we suggest that it hardly matters whether God's people worship Him or not all the year round, are we not selling God short and therefore selling people short? Is our vaunted compassion for all no better than wet and woolly? Honesty and integrity matter enormously too; so do we go back to the Pharisees, or at least appreciate them before we criticize them? They were the best representatives of God's people. They listened to His word. They were the labourers who bore the burden and the heat of the day. They were the elder brothers who stayed at home earning their living, not gadding about. But (this is the real point) even their goodness would not do, for the same reason that ours will not do: not just because it falls short; but particularly when it does *not* fall short, it seems to limit God. That surely is why Christ, when he came, had to go outside the enclosure of obedience because it had become an enclosure. People who uphold the Law easily slip into making the keeping of the Law a condition for God's favour. We uphold the Gospel, of course, but what Gospel? Sometimes we seem to say: repent and believe, commit yourselves so that the Kingdom can come. We ought to be saying: the kingdom of God is at hand, *therefore* you are given the chance to repent and believe. I find myself deeply suspicious of the associational church, not because it triggers off the word 'sect', which in the Church of England we have been taught to dislike, but because I am deeply suspicious of *human* commitment.

I meant to explain this with the help of the slogan 'justification by faith, not by works'. We don't earn God's favour: it is given to us. All we can do is respond. It occurred to me that justification by faith can be turned against me. It can easily be turned into justification by commitment! So faith itself gets made into a work. Surely it is better and more ecumenical to emphasize justification by grace: God's grace, which comes first. Both in the Old Testament and in the New Testament God's commitment comes before ours. He brings his people out of the land of Egypt before he gives them the law they are to live by. He sends his Son to live and die for sinners, not for the righteous. So indeed we have a call, and a call for commitment; but before that we have something which has happened, something to take our stand on, something objectively there which is God's doing, not ours. Of course this is exceedingly risky. It practically asks us to take it for granted, to neglect our part, to be ungrateful. 'He came to his own and his own received Him not'. But at least this beginning doesn't shrink the Gospel and God's new covenant with His people to some kind of conditional offer.

I don't know what kind of church we would try to set up if we were starting fresh like St Paul. We are not starting fresh; we have parishes. Nor do I know whether we ought to be content if the parish system were working well and making us complacent, if it were a great success. Maybe in those circumstances we ought to set about shaking it up a bit. It is not just making a virtue of necessity and special pleading, I believe, to find theological sense in what we actually have: churches that people belong to and neglect, churches that people come to when they want something. Are they saying to us what the parable of the prodigal son has been saying all along? The younger brothers in the far country get hungry and dissatisfied and come for nourishment. The father kills the fatted calf, the elder brothers are bothered. In taking the risks (which the elder brothers are conscious of) with open eyes and making people welcome when they don't deserve it, the church is surely reflecting divine reality. In saying this am I trying to make commitment pointless?

There is a recurrent problem here which I have nicknamed the problem of butter and margarine, the problem of tolerance at odds with excellence. It is beautifully put in Dorothy L. Sayers' *Murder Must Advertise*, where her hero is learning how to be an advertizing agent and he says, (trying to write slogans):

> . . . 'I see. Just something about "Better than Butter and half the price." Simple appeal to the pocket.''
> 'Yes, but you mustn't knock butter. They sell butter as well'.
> 'Oh!'
> 'You can say it's as good as butter.'
> 'But in that case,' objected Mr. Bredon, 'what does one find to say in favour of butter? I mean, if the other stuff's as good and doesn't cost so much, what's the argument for buying butter?'
> 'You don't need an argument for buying butter. It's a natural human instinct.'
> 'Oh, I see.'

I certainly can't claim to have solved this problem. On the contrary, I want to draw your attention to it for discussion as one of the great recurrent problems of our lives. How can we do justice to excellence without making excellence into a tyranny? This problem crops up again and again everywhere. But in our immediate context when the excellence we are talking about is 'commitment', there is something we can say. We need not hopelessly juggle with 'the committed are the best', alongside 'of course, the others are just as good'. We don't have to be complaining or uncomplaining elder brothers, or for that matter claim our rights and go off to the far country and come back when we feel like it. What we can do is ask, what is Christian commitment for anyway? And then the answer becomes obvious — surely it's for the sake of everyone else? The elder brother would have been fine if he had stayed put for the sake of the whole family. The committed are not 'the goodies' rather than 'the baddies', the excellent rather than the passable, but the foundation rather than the superstructure. To put it naïvely, we might imagine the Lord saying, not 'these are the choice few', but 'I'd better make a start with these. These are the ones that happen to be handy'.

Let me commend to you a concept which I very much like and have quoted in various places in various contexts, the concepts of an elder theologian, O.C. Quick — the principle of representative dedication. This comes in his book *Essays in Orthodoxy*.[1] He is discussing primarily the relationship between religion and the rest of life. The part of our life, anybody's life, committed directly to God is generally and perhaps ought to be a tiny proportion. Instead of saying, it ought to be bigger or it ought to be the whole lot, what we should do, he says, is look upon it as representing the whole.

Sundays and churches are not nearer to God or more excellent: they are fractions, set apart to represent the truth, he says, that all time and all space are God's. The part is consecrated, not instead of the whole, but on behalf of the whole. So perhaps we can say, the committed are not more excellent but representative of the whole. And indeed, Quick does say this about religious persons. Religious persons are not supposed to be more holy or more godly; they are supposed to express the holiness and the godliness which is everywhere (and the chapter in which he writes this is called, 'The Sanctifying Spirit'). And likewise might we even dare to say that commitment is somehow a special vocation?

For the commitment which is due from all of us, which I don't want to belittle by any means, I prefer the concept not of commitment but of *practice*. I have put this in print recently in a contribution to, *Crossroads are for Meeting*, from which I will quote.

> If perfection really is our goal, it is not commitment that makes perfect but practice. A practising Christian is as definite and energetic an idea as a committed Christian, without the smug overtones. A beginner practising on a musical instrument can make some horrible sounds, not at all

agreeable at first. A lot of practice is needed to make heavenly music. A children's concert is delightful to proud parents, but hardly to connoisseurs. What we are promised is that one day we can be good enough to tune our harps for God's own pleasure; and God is the proudest of parents and the most exacting of connoisseurs. Meantime we may well suppose that a Christian minister can better be compared with the conductor of a band than with a swimming instructor wondering whether to induce shivering bathers to jump in by wheedling or pushing.[2]

At least we can say this. We are all, committed or not so committed, on the same footing of mercy, which we cannot earn but to which we can respond. The heart of the matter is this, that what God is like is not something we can make up for ourselves, and if indeed God is real it is not for human beings to make the conditions. What has been entrusted to us, and it is a lot, is to make the real God more or less findable to one another, and that is what we need to be discussing. I am not trying to say the parish church is doing this well, only that it has made a start by being there, by having this objectivity which we believe that God Himself has; by not picking and choosing; by offering the grace of God to His ungrateful people. It is not something we ourselves make by joining.

This word 'findable' is to me something of a key word. I would like to stress that it is hard to find God. Human beings keep on seeking, and in the twentieth century we are getting more and more aware that science can't find him in the gaps. We are also getting increasingly aware of the problem of evil. I think it is much harder now that we have got the modern democratic idea which has given us a much stronger feeling that the world ought to be fair. Once upon a time when God was our absolute monarch we didn't think He was expected to be fair. He would give one lot of people horrible lives and another lot lovely lives, and this was the way He had chosen to do it, we just had to obey. Now we think the world ought to be fair, and that democracy is the right way to run our political lives; we therefore do find it very much harder than our predecessors to believe in a good providence at all. It isn't the dreadful things that happen to us, but the dreadful things that happen to other people, many of which don't seem to be much to do with sin. Therefore we can't easily find God in the course of events. For myself, were it not for the life, death and resurrection of Christ, I should have to say I cannot find God in the way the world is. The coming of Christ, the incarnation, is to me what makes the difference between God being findable and not being findable. This embodiment of God, the word made flesh, is literally crucial. There may be lots of ways of finding God. I am not trying to rule out other people's ways. I am not trying to be unecumenical about other religions. I am saying that this is our way, and it is an exceedingly significant way.

But then of course we have to ask, how do we find Christ? I am Protestant enough to want to say, in the Bible, but we have to be very careful. What we have to keep on saying is that the Bible is the Church's book. We can't take the Bible apart from the Church. The Bible, we know, is human beings, as much as the Church is human beings and partly the same ones. We are not, however Protestant we are, going to outgrow our dependence on other people.

Whatever else we are going to say about the Church, whether we have a high or low view of the Church, it is surely the Body of Christ in the sense that it is there to make Christ findable. This is where I would want to criticize the parish, not the idea of parish, but the way the parish is at the moment. I just don't believe that a stranger dropping in on an ordinary Sunday service, or for that matter on a Christmas morning service or harvest festival, will easily find what as Christians we hope that he or she is really seeking.

Think, for example, of a factory worker whose wife is seriously ill. What could he find if he takes up going, in his troubles, to a reasonably prosperous parish church? Think of all the innumerable people who feel that church-going is for the good and the virtuous, that they haven't qualified to join this club. It is not the associational church that would help these, but the parish which ought to be able to, if the Christian community had some notion of Christian theology, that God has visited and redeemed his people. The point of church-going and the point of the Christian life is to say 'thank you', not to conform to a standard.

Of course all of this cuts both ways in relation to what is happening to liturgy at the moment. On the one hand we have got to say that what goes on in church must be 'understanded of the people'; but on the other hand this has been a disastrous time for such wholesale changes as have been made. When some members of the party are lost, the last thing the rest of the party ought to do is go off somewhere quite different. You do want to be still there if some of these prodigals actually come back; and if they come back and find the whole thing has completely changed, it is not going to make life any easier for them.

There is a recent editorial in the magazine *Theology*, by Peter Coleman, Bishop of Crediton, where he takes up the slogan which has been so welcome to many people, 'put people before buildings', and rather naughtily switches this round and says, 'what about putting buildings before people?'. He explains what he means by this: put buildings in front of people 'put temples', he says, 'in the middle of things'.[3] He presents this as a kind of little fantasy, but I think it is worth keeping in view. In some cases cathedrals have been able to do this perhaps more easily than parish churches have.

Another article in *Theology*, by Peter Kerr, says, 'what we ought to be doing is sensitively make available to people the more universally resonant symbols of the christian tradition'.[4] He suggests that we ought to look on ourselves as hosts. The church is the host, and our job is to offer people hospitality. We ought to receive, listen and also, indeed, confront with a distinctive presence.

This emphasis on hospitality leads on to the last thing I want to say, which is about sacraments in this context of God's welcoming availability. You might think that because I warm to folk religion and even to fringe religion, I would sit very loose to the sacramental side of Christianity. On the contrary, if the church is there to make God findable, it is there to keep people quite literally 'in touch'. Folk religion is not unsacramental. It sets a lot of store by outward visible signs by which we find another dimension to life;

white weddings, pumpkins in church at the harvest festival. These are physical symbols which are important to human beings; by comparison, it is exceedingly hard to keep in touch in a purely spiritual way. For myself, I couldn't do it, and I cannot believe that that is what 'worshipping in spirit and in truth' is meant to mean.

I have emphasized saying 'thank you', not for one's own good luck (the sort of special providences one likes to think one finds in one's own life), but saying 'thank you' according to the General Thanksgiving, for our creation, and preservation, and especially for the redemption of the world, the means of grace and the hope of glory. The Eucharist brings together *thanksgiving* and *means of grace* which are surely, whatever else they are, an appointed means of keeping in touch. Christ is known, as he was on earth, in the breaking of bread. Of course we don't understand all the ramifications of this, but what we have to do is 'take this'. I am particularly fond of the verse ascribed to Queen Elizabeth I (which I don't think is cynical):

> His was the word that spake it,
> He took the bread and brake it,
> And what his word did make it,
> I do believe and take it.

There are plenty of themes for development here, traditional themes like sacrifice, covenant, supper, communion. The two I am trying to pick up are the ideas of 'real presence' and of blessing, in the sense of consecration. I would like to take extremely seriously the idea of God as promising to be present, blessing and using *things* as pledges, literal pledges, of his presence. He can be present anywhere he likes. He is present in many places we don't expect; but there are holy places, where he has undertaken to be. If this is how we understand the Eucharist and all the other sacraments and sacramental things in our religion, we can be less possessive about this whole sacramental idea. We don't have to denigrate folk religion as unreal and unworthy when it wants, perhaps incoherently, sacraments as ways of expressing spiritual reality. Certainly when people come asking for rituals which become traditional (white weddings with all the trappings, christenings for their babies,) we can remind ourselves that what they are asking for are known means of grace. We ought to be exceedingly careful how we offer them something called 'a blessing' *instead* of this. Blessing is, surely, God's grace given to us, often through consecrated material things. It is not something *else* we can have, second best, if we don't qualify for the full rite. God of course can by-pass or overflow his own channels whenever he likes, and presumably if they are blocked he will. But heaven forbid that *we* should block them.

Let me end with an inconclusive word about baptism. If one believes in sacraments and cares about them, it is tempting to make baptism, rather than 'commitment', into our standing ground. Then we can defend the parish church model, as doing justice to the reality of baptism as what makes us belong to God's people; and anybody who is baptized has the right to come to the parish church. This of course is ecumenically very attractive too, because Roman Catholics are coming to think that if we are all baptized we all do belong to one church. There is a lot here to work on in this way, and it is being worked on. The trouble is that it only shifts the 'butter and margarine' problem along a bit. Because, of course, we want to be fair to the people who, through no fault of their own, aren't even baptized; the Quakers and so on, on principle, and others whose parents never brought them to the font. Can't they belong? So we either get legalistic or undiscriminating. We have to say, only butter is any good *or* this margarine counts as butter, *or* buying butter has no point after all. I certainly think that to say, 'all the baptized in the parish' is much better than, 'all the committed' or 'only the committed' — as long as it puts the emphasis on God's promises rather than on human works. It *can* turn, if we are not careful, into a sort of justification by other people's work which looks very like justification by chance. This one was baptized so he can be married in church and this one wasn't, so perhaps he can't be.

What I am leading up to is the dangerous but attractive notion that what makes us God's people is really and truly our birth not our baptism. We can say that it is our humanity that makes us God's people. So I dare to call myself a Christian humanist. The whole idea of setting up an earthly criterion for belonging sits very oddly with the Gospel accounts of Christ's ministry. We can never claim to have God's mercy taped. We mustn't minimize His demands, but we certainly cannot organize them.

7

Models of God

Ruth Etchells

Any understanding of the Church must start with a theological under-standing of God and of the Church, and use this to throw light on sociological perspectives. The relatedness which is at the heart of the Trinity is the ground of the relatedness between ourselves and all other parts of the Creation. God is power, but hidden power. These aspects of God find expression in the nature of the Church: besides the 'communal' and the 'associational', relatedness within the local church extends to a 'hidden' or invisible Church, identifying with what the Church believes.

Reading the discussion paper and previous seminar presentations, I note the pressure over the year to change the question from one of 'definition' — 'what is a parish church?' — to one of 'validity' — 'does society need it?', as the course of seminars has progressed. I suggest that one of the reasons for this drift in the question is because the questions raised in discussion during the year have been posed very largely in social terms, even when it is the Church's own attitudes we have been pondering; or in terms of humans relating to and in their society, either from within or outside their church.

But the discussion paper poses the question, expressed in its third paragraph, of the *double* context of its address:

We believe the fundamental *theological* issue underlying all this shift and confusion is God, His nature and His purpose. What is to be believed about God and His relation to the world? And within that relation, what vision does the *Church* have of its function? Stated in its sociological rather than theological terms, the question is to do with how the Church manifests its task as an institution *of* society and *within* society.

The phrasing of that last part of the paragraph above could confuse our sense of the true nature of the Church, and cannot easily be married with the first part of the paragraph. (Or at least it sets it in terms so constricting that they erode the crucial element of the Church's identity.) To refer in an unqualified way to the Church as an 'institution of society' could make us miss its very point. Like saying of Liverpool football team that they are a group of men in red shirts who give pleasure to thousands on a Saturday afternoon. The point is, Liverpool football team *plays football*: that is what it is about. The social resource it provides, and the consequences in families and districts and across the world; its cultic mysteries; its financial impact; its associated phenomena in law breaking and in inspiring aspiration, in supplying a home for the starved imaginations of youth in a grey and deprived city; these fascinating and powerful social effects are all secondary. *Primary* is the fact that it exists to play football.

And in the same way, the Church is about God. Its very nature depends on the nature of God. And its role as a force in society is secondary. Powerful, to be thought through, and demanding the most serious exercise of responsibility; but nevertheless secondary to that primary identification. (We see this the more clearly in societies such as China's, where the Church was not allowed to exist socially, at all, for over twelve years, but most definitely remained 'the Church'.) Although, in the paragraph I have quoted, reference is made to 'God, His nature and purpose', as the first of the two contexts of our study of 'what is a parish church?', not a great deal about God appears in the papers. About what in *our* need or hope we might expect of Him, or how *we* relate to Him, or (more sparsely) of what might be His activities in the world, yes, there is some material to provoke and challenge thought. But of His *'nature and purpose'* — particularly the first — there is, as Paul Daniels would say, 'not a lot'.

And that is in the first instance right, because the sharp freshness of insight has been in applying sociological models to questions and issues normally expressed only in 'spiritual' or 'religious' terms. Therefore we all need to be challenged by the freshness and sharpness of these before the next stage of our thinking, and I have found the models offered an immense help towards this next stage. That next stage must, for me, be the interpenetration of theology and sociology, of models of God and models of society. This interpenetration demands that we examine one or two *theological* models of the Church, expressing, that is, the nature and purpose of God, and hold these against the sociological models with which we have been presented. What models of God might help us to perceive the parish church *theologically*?

1 Our very concept of 'relatedness' is rooted in a Creation theology where God is *Creator* of all things — which are therefore related to each other *in Him, before they are related to each other in any other way*. My primary relatedness to my dog, Bonny, to such of my family as are still living, to my colleagues at work, to the Dean of Durham Cathedral where I

worship, and to all of you with whom I now engage, is that God created each of us and we are related thereby *in Him*. We have, I suspect, in the Church, rather frighteningly lost the immense force of the primary implications of that creation theology and yet no thinking about the Church can afford to ignore it.

2   This Creator God also expresses 'relatedness' within His very nature. That is the force of Trinitarian theology. By that I mean that Christians understand their God as not simply expressing 'solitary might', but as being within His very self an expression of that 'relatedness' which we also see as a law of all life as we know it. So, 'Father, Son and Holy Spirit', the Christian 'model' of God, is not simply some residual formula left over from dead theological disputations of dry-as-dust ancient churchmen. Instead it is a living statement of a truth about all life: the life of the world we inhabit and also of the heavenly world beyond and behind, of which we get glimpses through such revelations as scripture and prophecy and the life and death and resurrection of Jesus Himself.

3   This 'relatedness' which is the very core of God's nature and therefore of all life which He creates, finds its especial force in the work the Holy Spirit does for us. Traditionally, the Church ascribes its foundation to the Parousia, to the coming of the Holy Spirit upon Christ's followers after His Ascension. The event (Acts 2) was marked by *extraordinariness*, of which we get glimpses only, with phrases that try to catch likeness: 'It was, as it were, *as though*' – and there is the description of some force 'as it were' like 'flames' and 'mighty wind' and then a flow of *understandable* 'speech' (the *opposite* of Babel) and 'the Church' had suddenly both identified itself and gone public.

So the nature of God showing itself here at the birth of the Church, (from which all our discussions about 'the parish church' derive) is of a *power* which is mysterious in kind but which pours itself out by means of 'the Spirit' – *i.e. that aspect of God which is directly communicable to His creatures*. The *effects* of that power are identifiable within the attitudes and behaviour of the 'gathered group' who at that point become the newly born Church. They marvel, they praise God and declare His wonderful works, they are 'lit', and they rush out to tell the world around, or at least the bit of the city they are in. The model of God here is of the Creator acting both *upon*, and *through*, His people; and eliciting a response which is rooted in wonder, delight, thankfulness, release and new confidence.

4 But between that experience of the nature of God which gave rise to the new Church, and, earlier, the cosmos's experience of the nature of God which gave rise to its own creation, lay that outworking of the 'relatedness' at the heart of God which we call the 'Redemption'. And the whole 'story' of God's redeeming of Creation, expressed as Christians know it in the Incarnation, is a clue to another theological model for the Church. For an aspect of God's nature and work and purpose that we have to take seriously is its *hiddenness*. We have to make the difficult imaginative leap of abandoning hindsight, in order to recognize how almost totally 'hidden' was God in Jesus Christ until after the Ascension (though believers saw it, particularly with the resurrection — it became 'open' to them). To the unbelieving world the redeeming aspect of God's *nature*, its depth and magnitude, was hidden, as His redeeming *work* was hidden, in the poor and insignificant figure of Jesus bar Joseph.

And so we find the paradox: that the nature and the purpose of God are both 'open' and 'hidden', both as we know them in what He reveals of Himself through direct revelation, and in what He reveals of Himself through interaction with His world in general and with believers. Any discussion of the parish church must therefore take full account of this 'hiddenness'.

To sum up. Among the *theological* models available to us for this discussion are:

First the 'relatedness' which is at the centre of the Creator God's nature, which gives ground for any relatedness we feel each to other in Creation;

secondly, the 'mysterious power' which is a direct outpouring of God's nature upon His people through His Spirit, which elicits a response that is wholly delighting and releasing; and which gave birth to the Church;

thirdly, the paradoxical quality of openness and hiddenness which attends both God's nature and His purpose, and is characteristic, in particular, of His redeeming work in Jesus Christ.

It is important now to see how these theological models express themselves in the Church, and in particular in its local manifestation, in Anglican terms, the parish church.

Insofar as 'relatedness' is of the very nature of God, it follows that His people share that nature. I would want to use this theological concept to interact with the social concept presented to us of 'relationships and relatedness' (which I found most helpful) and I suggest that there is perhaps a third 'model' of local church we should be looking at, which is neither quite the 'parish church' ('communal church' in later papers) nor the 'associational church' we have been contrasting with each other up to now.

For since our 'relatedness' is not simply territorial (*i.e.* defined by parish boundaries) but something inherent in our created nature, it follows that three kinds of 'bonding' take place within the parish. (By 'bonding' I refer to the psychological concept in which strong interconnections *form* between persons which make their mutual histories intertwine even should the people themselves be separated.) The three kinds of bonding that are happening in a parish are: *first*; that of proximity: a common terrain forges a (possibly quite slight) mutuality of interest: this is primarily a *social* phenomenon. *Second*, that of 'relatedness' in the sense in which I have been using it: as primarily a *theological* phenomenon (though social forces strengthen this). *Third*, that of 'belief'. And this relates to the third of the models of God's nature of which I spoke, that of its openness and yet its hiddenness. Let me explain.

Bishop Geoffrey Paul wrote to his ordinands as he lay dying in hospital: 'the world, the world, the world is redeemed: do you *believe* it?' Believing it is what Christians do: it is what defines them. It is 'belief' that must define them because much of 'redeeming' is even now hidden: not public, not 'open'. So, the local church is a group of people who come together in belief, to give public voice to that belief and its implications for them and for the world.

But beyond that public group in the local church is a much wider group of 'believers' who are nothing like so specific in their belief, and certainly are not going to be public about it; but who do believe that God is a good and gracious God whose will for the world is benign, and to whom Jesus Christ stands in some relation which expresses that goodness. These 'hidden' believers form a wider community of belief than the open, public members and active adherents of the local church. Their 'bonding' in belief is much less strong, but it is still real. And it certainly should not be disregarded.

We need therefore to talk not only about the *visible* local church and whether it is 'communal' or 'associational'; but we must talk also about the *invisible* local church. And this immediately changes to some extent the categories of 'communal' or 'associational' since neither of them quite fits.

For the local 'invisible' church is not necessarily identified either with the 'growth of the local church', nor with 'a concern for ministry to all members of the community'. It is more likely to see the local visible church as a material expression, which on the whole it does not find particularly attractive, of 'belief' which it holds fairly vaguely but quite deeply. It regards the local church as a group of people who perhaps take over-seriously, and who seem to give too much time to, belief that ought not to take such time and hard work. But it matters that the local church is there for the *public* expression, at life-crisis moments, of those beliefs: in baptisms, funerals and weddings. All this is quite close, I think, to the 'idea in the mind' in the discussion paper. (cf page 5)

Finally, my second 'theological' model needs looking at. The analysis of the local church, communal or associational, seemed almost entirely human-centred in the original document, *i.e.* the vision and direction and dynamic come from the human beings making up the church.

But the force of the theological model is to turn the question round and express it in terms of: what power is God pouring out in the local church? What is that power doing? What is that power shaping? and perhaps, even more profoundly, the question should be not 'Does society need the parish church?', but 'does God require of us a parish church?'

Tony Dyson in a memorable paragraph has described the function of the visible Church thus:

> Without the Church . . . how shall the faith, hope and love of the Christian community as God's gift be together affirmed and celebrated, how shall Christ's life and teaching be recorded and transmitted for others to know and obey, how shall members of the Church individually dispersed throughout the world receive spiritual nourishment and support, except there be an outward and visible institution which publicly witnesses to Christian belief, publicly witnesses to God's concern for the poor and needy, and publicly witnesses to the work of God in human history?[1]

I have deliberately spent my time on the *theological* models of the Church Tony Dyson touches on here, rather than the social ones, in order to further this next stage in the interpenetration of the two ways of thinking. And I would suggest that my own 'notes for further work' would pick up the two concepts expressed in the discussion paper, 'the church and the community', 'mankind and God', and work at how those two concepts intermingle.

In conclusion, some individual points in relation to the discussion paper. Neither the 'associational' nor 'communal' models fully express, I think, what the local church *receives* from the local community as well as *gives* to it. At best it is enriched by the tide of daily life, of ordinary hopes and fears, joys and derelictions which wash in and through it because of the life of the community in which it is set. The *version* of corporate worship in the parish church seems very human centred! Does not the worship, have at its centre not man but God: indeed, is worship not the language of humankind both *to* God and inspired *by* God, rather than *by* humans *to* humans about God?

I found the phrase 'feel real' on page 11, as an effect of members 'bringing their good and bad parts into the church itself' something of a questionable value-phrase, since associational churches who 'project' their 'bad' out on the world also 'feel real' — *very*, in fact! I wonder how wise it is to make 'feeling' a criterion at all?

However, I liked the following sentence, immensely: 'The importance of liturgy in the parish church, and the centrality of Holy Communion, is that they sustain the *spiritual* and psychological reality of this dynamic' (page 11). But I would want to add that liturgy is the work of the *people*, not only of the clergy, and insofar as it is projected onto the clergy, something is being missed.

8

The Associational Church and Its Communal Mission

John Tiller

Both pastoral experience and theological understanding of the Church argue against the 'communal' model. A communal approach to the Church's mission to its neighbourhood can and should be combined with an 'associational' basis for membership. The Church of England has become stuck with a sacerdotal view of its ordained ministry, but experience of lay people in ministry and the prospect of distinguishing between a local ordained ministry and stipendiary 'outsiders' offers hope of a move towards a shared ministry.

I notice that the list of contributors to this series has two curious absences. One is a representative of a church which gives autonomy in ordering its ministry to the local congregation, whether it be Congregationalist, Baptist, Brethren or Pentecostal; the other is someone who is currently on Anglican parish priest. I am in no position to supply either deficiency, but the case which I wish to argue will relate to both of these dimensions. I intend to reflect upon my experience of working in a parish in Bedford between 1973 and 1978. The relevance of this example lies in the fact that, for a town parish, it offered an almost ideal opportunity for the development of a communal model of the Church as described in the introductory paper. In the event, however, I was driven to regard the Church as having certainly a communal approach to its mission, but requiring an associational basis of membership in order to fulfil it.

Unlike most town parishes the one I am describing had some sensible and realistic boundaries: the inner ring road of Bedford to the north and east; the river to the south; and at the inner end of the parish towards the town centre there was the borderland between residential family units and 'bedsit' land, where big Victorian houses had been converted into flats. The parish had its own local shopping centre, its own lower school and a middle school, a park for recreation near the river, and the basis of a very settled population which had received a very interesting mix in recent years.

The housing in the parish was divided into three distinct areas. First, there was the old terraced housing where some families had lived all their lives, and indeed one could still find two or three generations of the same family living in different houses in the same street. Since the sixties the population in the area had become varied by the arrival of various ethnic groups including Italians, East Europeans, Asians and West Indians. Then in the seventies, when the new housing estates in Bedford were getting further and further away from the town centre, these streets became very popular with young married couples buying their first homes, who found these solid and cosy little dwellings cheaper and more convenient than the new estates with their poor amenities and lack of a settled community. The second area contained pre-war semi-detached houses occupied by the original owners for the most part, now retired and having grown-up families who had mostly married and left home to live elsewhere: a middle-class, middle-aged and elderly district where the quiet streets contrasted with the life and noise of the previous area. Finally, on the opposite side of the main road going into town through the parish, there was a modern housing estate built on an old nursery where the Laxton apple had been developed. Some of the old apple trees had been left in the open spaces of this complex, which had won an architectural prize for its design and contained everything from sheltered accommodation for the elderly to starter homes and five-bedroomed detached houses.

So here was a neighbourhood which was very mixed, but at the same time had a definite sense of its own identity for reasons related to geography, to local amenities, and to the continuous life of the community which had always been changing but had never suffered serious disruption. And the parish church stood at the very centre, on the main road, where the three housing areas met.

Eighty per cent of the membership of this church was drawn from the parish. Its involvement in the community was quite extensive, and increased as time went on. We were able to build a new church hall complex attached to the church, and to begin community activities like a playgroup for youngsters in the area, a mothers and toddlers group to welcome new families moving in, a senior citizens' lunch club, and English classes for some of the non-English speaking Asian immigrants. The extent to which this church was seen as a communal one was illustrated at the time of the Queen's Jubilee, when one street opted to move into the church hall for its street party. Moreover, when parents at the lower school were worried about an education policy of moving their children to a different middle school, the parents' action group instinctively asked me as the parish priest to chair the meeting which they called.

I have described this particular situation because I now wish to recount four experiences which put a qualification against this whole concept of the communal church.

The first experience was when I visited a man who lived almost opposite the church in one of the terraced houses. He remarked: 'Of course, the church is not for the likes of us.' He expressed *the alienation of the working class* from the Church of England. One had to recognize that there was a Baptist church in the parish which had grown out of the desire of the working class *not* to be associated with the Church of England. It had for many years had a much more effective Sunday School in the neighbourhood than the parish church and it had its own historic place in the community. Of course that place was no longer distinctively working-class, but the associational basis of the congregation remained and this in no way prevented it from having a communal role.

Next I recall the occasion when I visited someone from the modern housing estate, a man who drove past the church every day on his way to work. I introduced himself as the vicar from his parish church. 'Oh really, where's that?' was his response. He had never even noticed the building, nor had the thought that he belonged to a parish entered his head. He expressed *the rootlessness of the mobile class*. He did not expect to remain in the area long, and it would have been too painful for his family to get too involved in the community. He did not think in terms of belonging to a neighbourhood, but to a network of family and friends and the different worlds of business, leisure, and his home which was like a space capsule or a caravan temporarily parked in our parish. He was off most weekends, visiting his mother in a nursing home over a hundred miles away. We were irrelevant to him.

Then I went to see a bank manager who had just moved into one of the five-bedroomed, detached houses. I had received a letter from his previous vicar because his teenage children had been very keen members of the Pathfinder group in his church. As we also had a Pathfinder group there was an obvious point of contact. In this case I found that the man had opted to take his family elsewhere than to his parish church. The reason was fairly obvious. He was expressing *the discrimination of the rising class*: he, as a newly appointed bank manager, would meet much more important people, commanding much more important accounts, in the much more affluent parish next door. It has been correctly observed that the parochial system would have an opportunity of working only if it were compulsory. Once the possibility of obtaining all the rights and privileges of church membership by choice through electoral rolls had been introduced the parochial system, at least in the towns, was in effect destroyed. Possibly this did no more than adjust the church's structure to social realities, but it prompts us to question how far the communal model for the church is a hangover from the past.

This suggestion is reinforced by my final experience. One afternoon as I was walking down a street in the parish I found a friendly Italian at his front gate. He had no English, but we managed to converse in sign language with a bit of broken French. We were soon joined by another man who was the deacon in the local Ukrainian Uniat Church. We then went inside the house and had a splendid time drinking Stregas together, and communication got better as the afternoon wore on! In Bedford, the Roman Catholic Church has English, Italian, Polish, Slovenian and Ukrainian Uniat congregations. In that room we accepted one another as fellow Christians, but we represented *the plurality of ethnic groups* which was visible on the streets in that part of the parish at any time of day. Each group had a strong cultural identity and corporate outlook. It would be hard to pretend that this did not seriously affect, even if it did not demolish, the capacity of the Anglican vicar to be the focus of a communal church.

Now these observations are based on the experience of working in what was the most suitable parish in Bedford for the development of the communal model. The other parishes were in a much less favourable position, partly as a result of the way in which they had been divided up since Victorian times. The Church of England had gone through a process of having to put up new buildings to compete with the local chapels because people preferred to worship locally. But each of these daughter churches had aspired in time to become an independent parish. This was not just a matter of status: it was a way of securing continuity of ministry at a time when pastoral work was largely the preserve of the clergy; it was also perhaps seen as required by the communal model. As a result, the town-centre churches suffered. By the early seventies, four of the seven Anglican church buildings in the centre were redundant. Their boundaries were in every case unworkable and they relied on eclectic congregations. It was not simply that the population had moved: one parish consisted of a council estate half a mile away from its town-centre church. The result of this approach, which has created weak parochial units, has been isolation and even competition among the separate parishes.

This has been a devastating factor in much of the urban ministry of the Church of England. The communal model does not relate to the different levels of community and the vagaries of parish boundaries when it is applied to the non-neighbourhood churches which constitute the majority of urban congregations today. Moreover few of the town-centre churches have been able to address themselves to some of the broader communal issues as effectively as they might, because the whole thing is organized on a system of separate, self-contained parish units. There are signs in some places that it might be better to link together a town-centre church with a particular residential hinterland.

The question which this reference to a particular urban situation poses for us is whether the communal model of the Church is a hangover from a now outdated experience of the parochial system, or whether the parochial system is just one expression of the communal model which might now be replaced by other more effective versions of the same thing.

In seeking to answer this question, I believe that we must take cognizance of the fact that membership of the Church is always on the basis of individual association through baptism. Baptism is the way of joining the Church, theologically speaking, liturgically speaking and pastorally speaking. And baptism is required for exercising the rights and duties of church membership, even in the Church of England, although this has of course been obscured by the widespread practice of indiscriminate infant baptism — and also by the legal oddity that in theory a minister could probably be compelled to celebrate the marriage of two unbaptized persons if one of them happened to live in his parish. However, the Church and State Report of 1970 regarded this situation as quite unacceptable to Anglican theology, and so already the assumptions of the associational model were being taken on board by working parties producing reports for the Church of England.

Where this individual association through baptism has been obscured, the Church has tended to be seen as in principle the religious aspect of the culture in which it exists. And where the culture is changing rapidly, in its moral and religious values (and I think we can claim from church statistics alone that that must be so in our society today), the Church that is without an associational basis of membership becomes much more marginalized than one that has (unless there is outright religious persecution). As Valerie Pitt commented in her minority report to that 1970 Church and State Report, we may find ourselves identifying faith not merely with culture, but with a dying culture. This, it seems to me, is the greatest danger offered in the communal model today. It really has more to do with our cultural past than with our religious present. With which particular culture are we identifying? Is it a culture that is in principle nostalgic, related to the small, close-knit communities of the past? Valerie Pitt went on to say that our culture itself, as it grows away from its Christian roots, increasingly compels us to choose an allegiance.

It therefore seemed necessary, in the parish in Bedford which I have described, to keep the associational aspect of church membership steadily in view. We required of those who came, or brought children, for baptism, attendance at a series of preparation classes, a minimum attendance on three occasions at our monthly family service, and sponsorship from within the congregation in addition to godparents of their own choice. In actual fact we had very many candidates for baptism, because there happened to be a baby clinic just down the road from the vicarage, and I had only to mow the front lawn on a day when the clinic was operating to collect three or four candidates! We did not have a sectarian approach; we were quite prepared to meet the expectations which existed within the community, but on terms which expressed the associational basis of the church's membership. And this was further emphasized by the fact that coming to church more than once a month meant attending the Eucharist. During my time there, were only had one person who wanted membership without commitment to this limited programme, and during the last two years the majority of confirmation candidates were young marrieds who had first come into the church's fellowship through this baptism policy.

It is possible to argue on the basis of this experience that a local church may have a fairly articulate associational basis for its membership while adopting a communal approach to its neighbourhood mission. In Bedford we had as our objective, what the discussion paper speaks of as 'the spiritual well-being of the entire community living within the parish', including the society and the environment as well as the needs of individuals. All the points made in that paper were reflected in our communal approach to mission. But there is no reason why that cannot coexist with a coherent and positive associational basis for membership of the local church.

Finally, I would like to refer to what the paper says about the relatedness of the Church's ministry, and the particular place the ordained ministry has within the life of the local church. Again I suspect that it is our social and cultural roots which are governing our thinking in this respect, embedded as they are in the traditional role of the Anglican parson in the country parish — what Hurrell Froude called the 'gentleman heresy' of the Anglican clergy as the natural leaders of society.

Bishop Stubbs wrote before the First World War: 'There may come a time when candidates for the ministry must be sought from a lower grade and that very large sphere of the clergy as leaders of country society, prominently interested in all social movements, must be given up, their sole means of influence being the sacerdotal, their spiritual or ministerial influence. I do not think it desirable that such a time should be hastened.'

The Church of England has gone on thinking that it is not desirable that such a time should be hastened, but such a time has come and we are now left with a sacerdotal basis for relatedness, whereby the Anglican parson (or *persona*) is supposed, in the way the paper very clearly describes, to relate to the entire population of the parish for which he has been given spiritual accountability, no matter what its size may be or whatever possibilities for personal and individual relationships may exist.

This raises questions about our theological understanding of the nature of the Church, which is surely meant to figure the relatedness of all humanity in the interrelatedness of the different members of the Body of Christ. This common priesthood is inevitably overthrown by such a sacerdotal view of the ordained ministry. Whatever the theory, however, it is also a practical unreality in our present deployment of the Church's ministry, at least as far as the Church of England is concerned. Does this nexus between the parish and its priest require us to limit the number of parishes to the number of priests we happen to have available? Or is the answer to create sufficient priests to provide for every parish? At present we are in the curious position of having meaningless parish boundaries in the towns, although each parish may have its priest; while in the countryside, where significant parish boundaries often exist, we may have seven, eight, or indeed in one case as many as thirteen parishes in the care of one parish priest.

What about the possibility of ordaining a priest within each community? The Supplementary paper does raise the question of whether we ought to ordain people without even training them, and makes the point that as soon as we train people we change them. It is also true that as soon as we ordain people we change them. This focuses on the question of whether it is essential for the task of the ordained ministry that the priest be a man from outside, coming into the community as one who is able to bring together the different conflicts and tensions and needs within that community. In fact this is not how we have historically seen the Anglican ministry, which has in the past been a very settled ministry which has tended to work out its vocation within one very small community over a lengthy period of time.

Perhaps there are two needs which we have been trying to meet within the one ordained ministry. One is the role of the 'outsider', the person who is not identified with any particular in-group, but the other is the leadership of the local community. These two might very well receive a greater distinction in future. In a community which was able to do so, a local leadership might be produced which was recognized as being representative of the whole. I would want to argue that this leadership should be plural wherever possible, consisting of a group of persons, both men and women. It is the proper extension of the Parochial Church Council, created in 1921 merely to advise and co-operate with the incumbent, but now developing legal rights to determine matters which had previously been left to the parish priest. Alongside this local leadership, and providing it with additional resources and advice but not leading it, would come the stipendiary ministry, trained and deployed according to the needs, but definitely a ministry 'from outside', able to meet the spiritual needs which can be met only by such means.

Traditional expectations of the stipendiary ordained ministry as parish priests remain strong. But not for one moment should they be allowed to determine the future pattern of ministry, since they are founded on the assumptions of a cultural milieu which has all but disappeared. Moreover, these expectations can be changed and are in fact changing. Readers are now licensed to conduct funerals and I have met a lady in her seventies who regularly undertakes this ministry in her parish, including the counselling of the bereaved. It comes as a bit of a shock to people when they realize that she will be taking the service. But this ministry expresses her gifts, and that always wins through. Without exception people accept and gladly appreciate her sympathetic and understanding care, and the time which she is able to give. Through shared ministry by the laity, the Church is at last beginning to meet some of the expectations which have in the past been focused upon the clergy.

9

Whose Needs?

Peter Selby

The core group's paper has clearly touched upon a vital nerve, and yet the theory of the communal church needs to be radically questioned. It is difficult to ascribe meaning to, or to test, some aspects of the theory, notably the notions of projection and representation. It seems to function rather as a politically-motivated myth about both society and the Church, but the interests served by this myth are not made clear. A closer examination of the reality of society, by contrast with the 'society' referred to in the discussion paper, might point to the need for local churches which were more associational than at present, representing those groups who at present feel excluded or disenfranchised. At the root of the problem of association and community are the questions whose community, who decides, in whose interests?

As I left the house this morning my secretary said to me, 'I hope it goes well and I hope the answer is "yes".' That is, of course, because the words 'parish church' have imposed themselves on her consciousness. We ought to be clear, however, that what we are talking about is models and attitudes; we are not talking about the actual parish churches of the Church of England. I am glad about that, because my first reaction to the question is to put on my ecclesiastical-bureaucratic hat and say that the question is not, 'Does society still need the parish church?', but 'how many?' and 'where?'

Let me begin by mentioning a situation which will be familiar to very many people. The time is half-past nine in the evening. An exhausted couple are sitting watching the television, when they hear the sound of small, padding feet on the stairs. The door opens, and a little voice says, 'I need a drink'. Those of you who are familiar with that scene will also be familiar with the arguments which are then deployed. 'You've already had two', 'you'll be up all night', 'it will only make your little brother want one as well'; and finally, 'I told you to lie quietly and go to sleep'. In the end these arguments usually fail; the drink is supplied, not because the parents have become persuaded that there really is a need for a drink, but because they have become quite clear of *their* need for a quiet evening.

Does society still *need* the Parish Church? I have been interested for some years in the field of linguistic analysis. So I would like to try and examine what it is that we are being told in the discussion paper which was circulated to us. What is this theory, what is its status, what does it purport to be saying, and what does it actually say? What is happening when this theory is advanced?

The theories which are reflected in this discussion paper have touched upon a very raw nerve in the Church; that nerve is, roughly speaking, the debate between the sectarian and 'Churcharian' options for the Church's mission. That debate is going on all the time. On any day I could probably produce two or three examples from my work of the way in which the debate is coming up, mostly representing a very strong push in a sectarian direction. The other day a clergyman said to me that he was not going to conduct a wedding for two people, on the grounds that they were living together. When I pointed out that this would reduce his work-load of weddings quite substantially if applied across the board, he was not impressed, and he was not even impressed when I said that I thought the real logic of his position was to do the wedding quickly! The debate rages all the time, partly because of the institutional pressures to which the paper draws attention, and under which the Church currently labours.

But how shall we decide if society still *needs* a community church? How shall we answer this question? Some few years ago, the parish church of St John, Bedford Hill, Balham, was declared redundant. In the intervening period, there has been a quite marked increase in the incidence of kerb crawling in the area. Is this to be taken as an indication that somebody needed the community church? And how would we assess the causal or other link between these two phenomena? As I said right at the beginning, if you answer 'Yes, society does still need the community church', there is still the question about how many, and where?

Where I live and work there are parish churches within such close proximity to each other that you can see one from the next. There are places whose existence is being vigorously defended on the grounds of all kinds of needs which are not being met and which they need to be there to meet. Some of the needs are the kind of needs which are expressed in the core group's discussion paper. Some of them are quite different. I mentioned the redundancy of St John's, Bedford Hill. The issue raised there is the issue of the Balham Youth Centre Association's desire to have a place in which to meet. They are dealing in quite a different kind of need which, in their judgement, we should be supplying by letting them buy the church. I mention that because 'needs' are very slippery things. If we are going to make statements about society still needing the community church, we shall have to get a lot clearer than I think we have managed to get so far, about what the needs are that the community church is supposed to meet. Who decides that society needs them, who decides that it is the parish church that they need, and who decides that the needs which the community church is alleged to be meeting are in fact needs that ought to be met? These are all questions which arise when your child asks for a warm drink in the late evening, but they seem to me to be even more difficult to handle when we come to a social-psychological theory of the kind we are being presented with.

The issue is further complicated by interests. In whose interest is this question being answered? I could draw particular comfort and encouragement from the discussion paper, because of the much more interesting and enhanced role bishops are given if we believe that society needs the community church. Many of my colleagues are fond of saying that of course, it is important that they should spend time with the good and the great discussing important issues of state, and this has a real relation to the mission of the Church. How do we assess these attitudes? It is very easy to send up what is said here about representativeness. I was tempted to say that after my holiday this summer, I was going to enjoy asking people whether *they* were refreshed because of *my* holiday!

What all this adds up to is the question, what is the status of this theory we are presented with? I suggest that this discussion paper is actually a campaign document. What is happening is that a group of people, who work together in a particular field, have got together to provide ammunition in the campaign against sectarianism. I am bound to say that I think the comment in the supplementary paper, that one is not saying that the community church is better than the associational church, is disingenuous, because that is clearly what is being said; the form of the question dictates that. There is no reason why we should not discuss the question, 'Does society still need the *associational* church?' As the people who have made biblical contributions to this discussion have pointed out, Christianity began in a clearly associational frame of reference, not as a result of any particular decision, but as a result of the situation in which they found themselves. So the question, 'Does society still need the associational church?' would be just as germane, and it is important and interesting to notice that it is not the one that is being asked.

Another question concerns the word 'still'. Was there a time when it was clear that society needed the community church?

That question begs a further question, which is, 'What is society?' One of the aspects of this discussion is that we ask that question in the context of a highly disintegrated society, and of course that point is drawn attention to very carefully in the paper with which we were presented. Society is disintegrated, and it is suggested that that is one of the needs which the community church is still able to meet — the need for integration, the need for focus. But if society is, in fact, in that state, is it meaningful to ask questions about 'society' at all? Are not all questions about society actually questions about people in power, people with strength, people who are articulate, people who make the running? That is a running theme in my reactions to this paper. In whose interest is all this being said? In whose interest is all this operating, for whose sake, at whose profit, and at whose expense? These are questions which, it seems to me, need to be raised with regard to this theory. Let us be clear. What is being said to us is not that the Church should be community-oriented, that it *should* be a community church in the terms in which the theory describes that, but that it actually is. The theory purports to describe what is going on, that society needs the communal church and that there are various signs that it isn't getting it. And it is suffering because it does not have it. At the heart of this theory lies another theory to which I would like now to give some attention, and that is the theory of projection.

I don't criticize what this theory says from any great height. In my book *Liberating God*, I made considerable use of notions of projection and representation. I suggest, however, that when we are understanding projection as it figures in a theory of the kind with which we are being presented, we have to ask ourselves the question, what is the *status* of statements about projection and representation?

The concept of projection emerges from a clinical situation, where extensive use is made of it. Projection is brought about in order that the patient can experience the healing that results from handling what is actually the inner dynamics of their own mind — material which can't be handled in isolation, but which they can handle when they project it onto the screen of the other person. In the clinical context the notion of projection has had enormous value; that is well documented, and I add my personal testimony. It has been clinically useful to show the way in which people can produce in another person something from inside themselves.

As a result of that, it has also been found to be very useful in the understanding of small groups, where the behaviour of individuals within the group can be understood by reference to processes within the group itself. It has been found helpful to draw attention to the way in which particular individuals are manifesting in their behaviour certain characteristics of the group as a whole.

That, as I understand it, is what projection is all about. Let us be clear that in both the contexts which I have described, no attempt is made to determine whether projection is actually happening. It is enough that it is useful to think about the situation in that way. It is sufficient that we find it illuminating, clinically and diagnostically helpful in terms of people's learning about small groups. Words like 'helpful' and 'illuminating' are much more appropriate in evaluating projection than questions of truth. But I think we are entering another world altogether when we seek to apply that theory either to large groups or to the 'macro' processes of society at large. What we are then doing is making statements about what is going on which are extremely difficult to assess, as well as linguistically unclear.

If I say that the people who rioted on the streets of Brixton were representing something which was being projected onto them by all the other worthy residents of the patch which I oversee, how am I going to respond if somebody says; 'Well, how do you know? I don't feel in any way responsible for what has been going on in Brixton. I may be responsible in the sense that I voted for a government which has denied the Borough of Lambeth resources, and that may have some relation to what has happened in Brixton. But if what you are telling me is that my anger was somehow being manifested on the streets in anger against the police, even though I am strongly in favour of the police, (who are also incidentally probably manifesting my anger against the rioters), how am I going to know whether what you are saying is true?' How is Mrs Thatcher to be persuaded that Arthur Scargill is in some way actually representing her? How are we to understand these processes as operating? The theories we are being presented with treat the notion of projection in an almost mechanistic sense. If I project a projectile, that has a clear meaning in physical terms, and is clearly assessable. If I ask whether I am sufficiently projecting my voice in this room to be heard, that again is assessable. But if I ask if I am projecting my anxiety onto the members of this group, so that if anxiety comes out in the discussion it is traceable to me, we are in an area where I think assessment, evaluation, let alone verification, become very difficult.

The conclusion to which you are forced if you look at projection in that sort of way is either that projection happens all the time, because anything that anyone does is the result of things that other people project onto them; or it operates none of the time, and perhaps none are true. It is noticeable that when the paper seeks to define 'projection', what it says is, 'projection happens when people project' — and I sympathize with the core group's difficulty. So what *is* projection? What I'm going to suggest is that projection is actually a myth. You can get into serious trouble about using the word myth if you are in my position. What I mean is that a myth is something which purports to describe the world of fact, but describes it in ways which can't be checked in principle, though they make sense within the subjective observations of the people who hear it. Projection is extremely illuminating as an idea, but it has to be used with great care when we are talking about the 'macro' social situation. It really isn't clear whether it applies to everything or to nothing; because of that it raises difficulties about the whole theory which we are addressing at the moment. 'Does society still need the community church?' Are all the people who are attending the parish churches of our country somehow representing their friends and neighbours, and how will you decide whether they are or not?

The paper mentions the possibility that a congregation thinks of itself as a communal church, when actually nobody around thinks of it that way. It is certainly possible for a congregation to assume that it is purely associational, when actually there are aspects of the life of the community which the community expects to be reflected in the parish church.

What is going on? What does the theory say is going on, and what is actually going on? I have no doubt that if the Fellows of King's College, Cambridge, decided that next Christmas Eve, the Nine Lessons and Carols would not take place, let alone if they decided to put a false floor half way up King's College Chapel and make it into offices and lecture rooms, there would be a national outcry! This would be taken as evidence that something that happens in King's College Chapel is the result of projections by society as a whole. But is it? My hypothesis is that within a few years nobody would remember, or rather, that it would take guided tours to remind you what used to happen in King's College Chapel. And of course King's College Chapel is only one extreme example; Westminster Abbey may be another one.

Even in regard to those extreme examples the evidence for the projection and the evidence for the need actually declines over time, at least in its overt form. That is, the children do in fact go to sleep after a while. Is that evidence that they did need the drink, or that they didn't need the drink, or that they could get by without the drink but that they would have been better off with it? What conclusions are to be drawn from the fact of an outcry at one moment, and a gradual decline in expectations after a time?

My most recent experience of trying out my own view that there is some sort of relationship between the Church and the community, which cannot be lightly disregarded, arose when one of the Anglo-Catholic churches in my patch decided that since they were using the lectionary of the Roman Catholic Church anyway, it would be more convenient to distribute to the congregation the Pope John Paul II Missal, than to distribute copies of the Alternative Service Book or the Prayer Book. The result was, not surprisingly, a letter to the Bishop from a passer-by who went to the church for what he thought was the worship of the Church of England one Sunday, and was handed this document which was exactly what he didn't go there to get.

I raised the question with the vicar and the congregation. 'Do you think there is any contract between you and the public about what can go on and can't go on in this church, and do you think the Church of England is the guardian of that kind of contract, the guardian, in the sense of authorizing liturgies, and so on?' The answer was clearly, 'no'. They hedged a bit because they thought they ought to, but the answer was actually 'no'. They saw no such relation, an indication that in terms of the theory their attitude was totally associational. In their terms they were seeking to represent the universality of the Church in what they were doing.

But of course the person who came to the church took a very different view. Was he projected there, by a wave of feeling amongst the residents of that area? I find this frankly quite implausible. Was he there because he had been formed by the anti-Catholic strand in the British consciousness? Probably. How deeply ingrained that is is difficult to tell until one has a wave of anti-Irish feeling. How do we assess what is going on? I have said that what we are talking about is myth, myth that is more or less useful in pointing to meaning, or giving shape, giving understanding, telling stories which illustrate particular goings-on in particular places.

Beneath all of this lies a difficult question about the nature of community and in particular, who decides what is the nature of community, in whose interests it operates, who decides its shape and its meaning. My conviction is that there are large numbers of congregations in the patch with which I am most intimately acquainted who have a strong communal approach. It is precisely that communal approach which makes them most deeply suspicious of what is said in this theory to be the community understanding of the Church. They are communal, of course, in the sense that they believe in God's preferential option for the poor, in causing difficulty to the powers that be, in not simply meeting needs of the kinds to which this theory points but also the unexpressed need of a number of voiceless and inarticulate people for such a level of change in society as will enable those people to be incorporated into the community, in ways which they aren't at all at the moment.

Now I am someone who has always been strongly opposed to all the sectarian tendencies in the Church of England. I find that on most of the litmus test issues of sectarianism, such as baptism and marriage policy, I come out pretty clearly acid. But that does not answer the question of who the community are who might still need the Church. In order to support the community that might still need the Church because the community at present is not operating in its interests, we might actually have to be extremely associational. We might actually find ourselves excluded, disenfranchised, disliked, unpopular, precisely among those people who declare themselves to be most strongly interested in the community nature of the Church.

So at the root of the problem of association and community there is another question. That is the question, 'Whose community, who decides; whose power, in whose interests?' I believe we are being offered in this theory a psychological and sociological equivalent of monetarism. In monetarist theory, society will show if it needs the Church by whether it will pay for it. (On that showing incidentally it certainly needs far fewer than it has got.) Monetarism is a way of providing an index of need which has, I think, severe disadvantages, but does actually provide a way of measuring need. This theory seems to me to be suggesting that if there are community churches, it is because society needs them, and if they die it will be a sign that society does not. This matter can be settled by observation. The trouble is that, like monetarism, it operates very clearly in certain people's interests, and against the interests of certain other people. What poses as an entirely neutral understanding of reality is actually a highly politically motivated set of notions, which offer to the powerful and the strong enormous comfort. On that entirely uncontroversial note I end!

10

Working with Dependency and Keeping Sane

Wesley Carr

Society and the Church each need to be interpreted in terms of interactions rather than as definable entities. The Church specifically is an open system handling dependency and the irrational, and this is today all the more necessary in that society regards both with suspicion and disfavour. For this work the Church needs people in every place who can represent it and make its services available, while containing the pressures on them by setting clear boundaries.

'Society' is a very large notion. It is often used in popular writing and then refined in more careful and precise sociological texts. In this context, the word is used of something felt by anyone who lives in and contributes to groups and associations. In other words, use of the term directs our attention to experience, rather than definition. A church cannot determine what society is and what its needs may or may not be, and then plan a strategy. Society refers to something given, that we participate in and contribute to but which also comes at us and affects us, almost, so it feels, against our will. We need to hold the human perspective hidden in its use. For example, I was working recently with a group of YTS (Youth Training Scheme) boys. They, though largely illiterate, frequently used the word 'society' to describe their position. 'Society doesn't want us', or 'Society doesn't care', was a regular attempt to interpret their internal sense of futility and unimportance. Clergy experience a similar use when, for example, a couple, asked why they wish to marry in church, respond that it is the 'proper' thing to do. They do not know precisely why they wish to adopt this course, but they are aware that their lives, significant as they are to them privately at this moment, are lived in a public context.

When we use the word 'society' we need to get a handle on it, and for that I suggest the notion of *interaction*. This draws attention to the reality that the moment we refer to society in our thinking, we are not thinking of ourselves alone, nor of something wholly other, but of the messy world in which individuals and institutions have to orient themselves. The church, for example, in its local expression, does not just give to society or receive from society; the term 'society', like that of 'church', refers to a way of trying to identify something in an interchange which is inevitably unclear and uncertain. This is not very encouraging for those who wish to analyse everything into clarity. But it does mean that when we are thinking of institutions like the Church, we have to think in terms of dynamic activity, conscious and unconscious, and not just in terms of definable entities which can be identified. This is the bane of much contemporary thinking on the Church and its ministry, which tends to begin from within the Church, with certain assumed notions, and not to take account of the need to discover and, as best as may be, interpret these interactions.

An illustration may help. A recent enthronement of a new bishop was devised by church leaders with all the overblown pomp of the uncertain. The most chaotic moment occurred when the civic dignitaries welcomed the new bishop. Mayors and other leaders did not know what to say, when to say it or how to go about it. The assumption was that simply as people they would wish to greet the bishop. So he was described, of course, as *their* new bishop. No one had bothered to consult them about behaving in the roles with which they came. Without discerning the interaction, however insignificant, the Church imposed *its* models on confused people and left them both personally and in their roles publicly impoverished.

The question facing us, therefore, is what is the nature of this felt interchange and how is it to be interpreted? Where, then, is it felt and by whom? How do we get at it, let alone interpret it? These questions change our original one. No longer can we simply ask whether society needs a parish church. First we must ask, if there is to be a church, what forms it must take for any interchange to be noted, interpreted and used creatively. This is critical for all the churches today, not least my own — the Church of England. Without at least an attempt to address this question, our models of the Church and our theories of ministry will become removed from life as people live it.

To help us approach this question I wish to offer a more theoretical section, about which I hope people will ask questions and discuss. The approach to Church and society through the idea of interaction presumes two things: first, that the Church, along with other institutions, is an open system; and second, that a psychodynamic approach to interpretation is appropriate. Bruce Reed, and my late colleague Dick Herrick, have done sufficient work in different contexts to establish that it is legitimate to think of the Church as an open system, arguing more specifically that churches primarily function with the dynamic of dependency. But this needs constant testing. The essence of a psychodynamic approach is that theories and models are always themselves refined and changed by the use to which they are put. When, therefore, we look at the churches' interaction with other institutions and with 'society', we perceive that, as the definition of 'society' was problematic, so also is the definition of 'church'. Put at its simplest, the Church does not define itself but contributes to a dynamic of interchange which creates it. If society, therefore, in any sense needs the Church, then the Church will always in a similar sense need society.

Let us look more closely at these dynamics. Those familiar with group relations study of a large group will know the experience. It is disorienting, since the individual is trying to cope with a group of people which is larger than he can immediately comprehend. Things in which he is not fully caught up happen a long way away. Sub-groups emerge and disappear with bewildering rapidity. The individual feels isolated, unable or unwilling to participate. The world as known and trusted seems to have dissolved permanently into unrelated fragments. Bizarre behaviour, often accompanied by the threat of imminent violence to oneself or others, may ensue.

Defences are erected against this threat. Polarities, for example, are used to categorize sub-groups — consultants/members; black/white; male/female. But this usually only serves to contain strong feelings and then the next stage is reached — institutionalizing. Roles now become prominent and formalized. Management takes over and conservatism and tradition triumph. People are depersonalized and leadership ritualized, but so long as this is a temporary stage in the life of the group it can be useful, providing momentary respite from stress.

These experiences compare directly with what we today feel in relation to that other felt, but necessarily unencompassable 'other' — society. In society — by contrast with the temporary setting of a conference — this institutionalizing process goes on all the time. Somehow the psychological space between the individual and the highly significant but vague notion of society has to be managed, and this is done through the range of institutions available. The trouble at present is that in our preoccupation with institutions as they are, we overlook this aspect of their functioning. They provide foci for the individual's projections, and as such enable people to develop and sustain ideas which are crucial, if they are to find a way to negotiate the space between their individual and social existence. For they potentially provide a means of managing in a controlled fashion our inevitable regressions in the face of an imminent and threatening and incomprehensible power, such as society represents.

There is much more to this argument than I can give here. However, the problem should become clearer. In a simple society such regression can be managed ritually through an acknowledged institution, like a church, which provides ultimate security that the boundary between this life and the next, or between man and God, is managed. It handles dependency. But in our pluralistic society human experience is not homogeneous, and we must refine this dynamic notion of dependency before we use it too lightly.

Recently in Newham General Hospital I was waiting for someone and so read the notice board. It was loaded with notices about as many sub-groups as you can think of — racial, religious, sickness-based, etc. The cumulative effect, however, of all these groups vying for attention was to make me as an individual feel very excluded. Each notice began by welcoming and then ended by so narrowly defining membership that I almost felt guilty for not being something — black, Asian, female, carrier of this disease or that.

This story indicates two facets of this sort of society: first, its fragmentation into small, very limited but self-determined groups; and, second, the persistent sense that the world as a whole and as experienced in this fragmentation is impervious to interpretation. Both perceptions are important for our investigation into the parish church. Our experience of society is one of powerful sub-groups claiming rights and engaging in violent competition, sometimes creatively but not necessarily so. Alliances form but rapidly dissolve. They feel like a series of attempted pairings: 'If only we and they can get together', some hope can be sustained and something beneficial be produced. The pressure is to create links, and not to seek a dependable object.

This is a crucial issue: can two institutions, two groups, two cultures, even two people, be united to create something new, strong and hopeful? Any pair, however, although it may appear creative, also possesses innate potential for destruction and to sustain a pair a group inhibits its own potency. When pairing fails in a group, a familiar response is a reversion to dependence. But — *and this is crucial* — in a pluralist society a similar reversion can never occur, because this sort of society has pre-determined that its member-groups will be autonomous and highly individuated. This is a valued mark of such societies, without which they would not cohere. Consequently, dependency, however it is expressed, is inadequate as a holding dynamic. And a society in which dependency fails and which cannot mobilize fight for long, because without an external enemy this becomes internally destructive, may slip back further than we have usually recognized in our dynamic interpretation into a state of stasis, which is called oneness.

Oneness describes the second feeling that I have described — that the world is impervious to interpretation. When working with groups and organizations we tend to think of this as intractable dependency, as things get stuck beyond interpretation and we are unable to shift them at all. But this description is also worth questioning. Pierre Turquet, in his study of the large group, occasionally discerned a dynamic of oneness. In oneness, group members 'seek to join in a powerful union with an omnipotent force, unattainably high, to surrender the self for passive participation and thereby feel existence, well-being and wholeness'. But this language, you will have noted, is highly religious. Indeed, he goes on to speak of 'the mysteries'.[1]

If the prevailing dynamics of our pluralist society are the forlornness of pairing and the primitive regression of oneness, then an interesting but important shift is needed. In any society, those institutions which affirm Existence or the Mysteries — *i.e.* chiefly religious bodies — are those which are also customarily invited to handle dependency. There is a qualitative difference between oneness, which has to be affirmed, and dependency, which needs to be handled. To enable groups and individuals to move from the helplessness of oneness, the profundities of existence are first named and then made available for exploration. A key activity in this process, which involves a shift from one level of unconscious behaviour to another, is ritual. Here the churches may discover one of their distinctive contemporary tasks: that is, to enable dependency to be acknowledged, accepted and articulated. In our world dependency is widely regarded with suspicion and disfavour. The struggle, joining and separating between sub-groups, of the pluralist society discounts dependency of any sort, and autonomy, falsely understood as hard, manly independence, becomes all. But without dependence and its corollaries, a society will be denying so fundamental an aspect of itself and of its members that destructive behaviour would seem to be inevitable, if we ever dare use such a word of human behaviour.

We are now, therefore, moving to a position to be able to answer the original question from the perspective of the Church as an institution within contemporary society. Does *this* society need the parish church? The answer must be yes, but not because it *needs* (in any simplistic sense) the Gospel that the Church professes (that comes later). It requires some institutions that can confidently affirm that dependency is a legitimate expression and can be mobilized, so that people and institutions can break out of the despairing spiral of the prevailing dynamics. Responsible behaviour can then be confirmed in individuals and institutions. For that to happen (here I risk being prescriptive), it has to be exemplified in the Church.

I have to say, however, that I do not see many signs of the church being willing to do this deliberately or, as often hitherto in more confident times, instinctively. I directly attribute the marginalizing of the Church to its own unwillingness to risk this. At the moment, in the guise of rediscovery of pristine purity, the churches are increasingly conforming to the prevailing dynamics of our society. Baptism becomes solely a joining ritual. The struggle around marriage is surrendered to expediency. The eucharist becomes a social event — shaking hands is increasingly the focus of the rite. House churches, far from being primitive, often represent contemporary social attitudes — dinner at home with a few chosen friends. And working theology is left to the bishops, where all sub-groups project their negative aspects. They in turn see themselves falsely as a focus of a unity, which is pure basic assumption behaviour. When that fails, as it inevitably must, the Church becomes a set of warring factions of the pairing type that I have just described.

In the light of this theoretical discussion we can illuminate the concept of the parish church. Most discussion about the parish seems either to be historically based or reduced to humorous looks at some of the more glaring anomalies. But in my experience both approaches assume a position *a priori*: that the parish system and the parish church is not a useful contemporary basis for organizing the Church's work. This seems to me fundamentally wrong, both as a method and, as I will try to show, in its result. Too much of our current discussion about the organization of the Church relates, without examination, to questions about geographical boundaries. When we look at the origin and persistence of the parochial system, however, a number of interesting points emerge. First, the *paroikia* was dynamic from the first. Although geographical shape was given to these parishes, this was largely because there was no other option. Behind the arrangement, however, lie two important points: first, the availability of ministry with authority to people wherever they were. They were not required to conform to a pattern in order to enjoy the Church's ministry. The Church organized itself — albeit massively influenced (what else could it be?) by the prevailing social and political structures — in order to be accessible to people wherever they were. Second, in view of the demands of dependency, which is an exhausting dynamic setting for work, the boundaries were drawn to determine the limits of the bishop's and priest's responsibility.

A parish system (which should not be confused with existing parishes) still performs this function — at least in theory. It is designed to provide the Church's presence and ministry so that it is accessible to people in an authoritative way, and, since the clergy become crucial focal points in all this, to give them clear boundaries, without which they would go mad. One of my fantasies about the Bishops of Carlisle and Newcastle is that, when they travel to London, they cross every new diocesan boundary with a thankful 'Not mine!'

In our present world, the existing parochial system can be too easily ridiculed. And the sense of stretching the limited resources of the clergy can be over-emphasized. But this does not entail abandoning the parochial principle, even if the detail is adjusted. We have, as always, to trust people and risk living with their decisions. They will choose where they feel they belong and create whatever we mean by 'community'. They will also choose what use they wish to make of any particular church. Our job, however, is not to manage people, but to remain sensitive to them and specifically to sustain accessibility and (for reasons which I will shortly amplify) a sane clergy. We may be able to discuss this later. Size is not a primary criterion. It is a factor, but not the most important. You can have very large or very small parishes, according to the way we deploy for this task. And the focus of availability may take different forms according to different social requirements. Buildings, for instance, are more important in some settings than others, but they are not uniformly symbolic. Sometimes a priest on the spot is vital; at other times we need only to establish a notion in the mind. We might elsewhere have to make a strongly religious statement, and so overtly deploy some religious group like monks. And I suspect that the Church of England is impoverished at this level by not being able to deploy the difference between men and women in positions of authority. But so long as the task, as I have outlined it, is understood, the strategy will follow, and, in my judgement, without as great a problem as we sometimes fear. Our contemporary anguish — which leads to questions like the one we are addressing in these seminars — is more to do with task confusion than lack of strategy.

If you ask why we should do this, you raise a theological question about the Church. In this paper I have to take it for granted that if in any sense society needs a parish church, then we, as Christians, have good reason for responding to that need, without hope of pay-off but chiefly as a living statement of the grace of God.

One function of a parish church is to keep the clergy sane. This might seem either a selfish or at times hopeless intention, but it is organizationally significant. If the Church is to keep working at dependency – and I agree that in our present society this remains a task, but one that has to be perceived in the more violent and problematic dynamic settings of pairing and oneness – dependency has to be risked as something to be encouraged and affirmed, with all the attendant dangers that such a stance can lead to delusion. As David Hay remarks at the end of his book, *Exploring Inner Space*:

> I doubt very much that religion is about to die out. The awareness out of which it grows is too widespread for that. More dangerous, because more likely, is that it may continue to be isolated from the mainstream of modern life. Human realities which are resolutely ignored tend, as Freud pointed out, to return in bizarre and fanatical forms.[2]

The Church is not just in the business of handling dependency, which sounds reasonably comfortable (if problematic); it is also an institution which deals with some of the irrationality in a society. This is an increasingly critical issue for our society and therefore for the Church. The irrational parts of ourselves are expressed but not worked upon. Protests, for instance, are a familiar form of expression, but are not usually work. They become self-perpetuating, because they have a superficial logic, or rationality, to them. The growing range of therapies emerges as a way of enabling the individual to cope with the felt irrationality of himself and his world. But again, these do little or nothing to change the conditions of that world, and are self-perpetuating. I can only touch on these vast subjects and commend to you other reading. Bernice Martin's *A Sociology of Contemporary Cultural Change*[3] is a masterpiece of insightful common sense and should be read alongside Bruno Bettelheim's *The Informed Heart*.[4] Both, from different angles and disciplines, make clear that there is a wide range of contemporary experience which brings to the surface what has often in societies been hidden away – the irrational in all of us.

Religious institutions are always going to be involved here. The argument about whether religion is a delusion or not is sterile. But religion certainly professes confidently to live with and work on borders and, in a sense, as a borderline state. Borderline states lie technically on the edge between illusion and delusion, where the neurotic and psychotic coincide, and they are being widely studied. There is a spin-off here for understanding the Church, religion and society. Anyone who professes to believe in God in today's world is probably concerned to some degree about being thought foolish or deluded. This fear may even contribute to the present difficulty that the Church has in engaging with those who live in its shadow but do not turn to it. There is some accuracy in the perception that religion is like a borderline state. This means that churches will necessarily be to a large extent repositories of irrationality.

Every minister knows how amazing the irrational behaviour of a congregation and its members can be. It sometimes seems that, when in the church, otherwise sane people lose their wits. They go to the stake for unimportant trifles. The home of love and fellowship is a hotbed of bitchiness. Reason always seems to lose out to unreason. This can cause despair, until we recognize that such behaviour is not merely the product of church life and religious belief, but is also a function of the external roles that church people hold in the world. In other words, the more irrationality in society is not addressed, the more likely it is that it will emerge in a chaotic fashion inside churches. The issue, then, is not so much why church people behave in so strange a fashion, but, more importantly, how this experience can be acknowledged, interpreted and used for the benefit of that society of which the church members are representing part.

We may look at one particular instance as an example — the occasional offices. I am sure that in dealing with baptisms, weddings and funerals, the church is handling aspects of dependency — and rightly so. But such a description is not sufficient. In a recent television comedy an ordinary couple were sitting on a canal bank. The boy wanted to live with the girl. She wanted to get married. He agreed, but assumed that this would only involve attendance at the Register Office. But she wanted the full works, including church and vicar. He was less keen, chiefly because he thought he would have to break a lifetime's habit and wear a tie. They discussed why they should go to all this bother. Finally it emerged that all she really wanted was the words: especially 'till death us do part'. These for her would make the wedding. You can interpret this in several ways, not least as an expression of dependency. But behind this light-hearted discussion you can also hear other voices. The couple were not conforming to parental or peer demand. They felt, for all sorts of reasons, that their lives were out of their control, and they were caught up in transitions that were important to them but not to others. Wildly irrational feelings were stirred up in them, and they were seeking a way of handling these — and the church possessed the means, in this case the words.

This is a trivial example, which no doubt this audience can multiply and improve upon. The point I want to draw attention to, however, is that dependency is not merely something given, an inexorable part of human nature. It is itself dynamic — that is, it is mobilized or not, and in different fashions, according to a wider dynamic spectrum. If as a church we simply affirm that we are in the business of handling dependency, we shall also move to discussion about the precise organizational form that we need to adopt. We may then become fixed in certain limited models. The debate, for example, about the associational *versus* the communal models of the Church (which, incidentally I frequently come across in my travels around the Church of England) can restrict our vision as much as it may clarify things. These descriptions represent two discernible responses to the pressure of the dynamics of dependency. But that is only a start. Dynamics are interconnected. So if, for example, we are going to use this simple but useful distinction between 'associational' and 'communal', we should further ask what one style of church life or the other also indicates about the way that the Church is responding to its environment. If, say, a church is apparently communal in its orientation, it may be reacting to some expectation as well as creating its own model of ministry. Similarly, a so-called associational church is not merely determined by its own wishes or theological understanding. We need again to ask what such behaviour is also implying about its setting and its place within it. In other words, we need to be more specific and to recognize that each time we feel that we are caught in some dependent frame, we have to ask why, and what generates it.

In the sort of society that we are now creating, one vital function of the Church is to acknowledge the irrational. We have the means. Ritual in particular is an effective way of dealing with irrationality. It does not dispose of it, but incorporates it into a framework where it can serve a useful purpose. Worship, whether the regular worship of the congregation or the more diffuse experience of the occasional offices, too, is an opportunity for careful handling of this. It is a primary self-defining function of the Church and one which is also a point of definition for the non-member. Our theology and practice has not yet caught up with this. But if the Church could see this aspect of its task and try to work with it, several benefits would emerge. Our theology would be more interesting and lively. Our practice would be more self-critical. The work of the clergy would seem much more significant and worthwhile and their self-esteem would rise accordingly, (and in order to love others there has to be enough self-love). And, what is more important than all of these, people in our society would increasingly see their place not just in our particular society, which may be too small and too fraught for the large vision that is now thrust upon us all, but in an ultimate framework of God's world.

How does all this address our original question? That, as I have tried to show, is a dynamic question, and cannot be answered easily so much as continually explored. When we attempt to respond to it, then our theology and practice are called into lively question. Whether we decided yes or no, we shall be changed. I believe that there is a continuing place for churches in the contemporary setting, but we have to be more critical in locating ourselves at points where we can do something. That is the basis of organization of any parochial system. In order to work in our present-day environment, I suggest three points must always be taken into account. These apply to diocesan and parochial planning alike, not least because there must be congruence between them.

1 If we recognize that we are handling such powerful emotions as dependency and irrationality and acknowledging a borderline state, a first requirement is sufficient containment. For people to find the church accessible and usable requires that we provide some human access points, people who publicly take responsibility not for the Gospel alone but for the institution as well. These are clergy, men and women, whose function is on this boundary. This means at least modifying, and probably abandoning, a number of fashionable views:

Local ordained ministry — this concept does not sufficiently distance these people for them to be used. They may look fine from within the church, but in terms of dependency and irrationality they are not usable. And we cannot split the internal and external aspects of the public role of the priest by appointing some to work inside alone (mass priests).

The freehold — although inevitably abused, this (or something very like it) is needed to provide an assurance in the midst of confusion that can enable the priest to remain usable. The protection is historically from the whims of bishop, patrons and congregations, so freeing the priest from those anxieties that he is able to live with the appropriate anxieties of his position. Remove them and the priest is in trouble, because he has no other defences — status, money or the fifty-minute therapeutic hour.

Diocesan organization as support — by proliferating so-called support systems we are conveying a message to these clergy that they are incompetent. When they begin to feel that, they believe it; and if they believe it, they lose their sense of a significant role; and if they do that the laity will begin to question the church's need for them; and eventually people outside the church will find them unusable.

The differentiation between clergy and laity — this is too big a subject to go into at length. The new director of Network

Southeast on the railways has publicly realized the basic point: the customers are not his first concern, but his staff. All railway workers, at every grade, must be affirmed in their general role as railway people and in their specific role as porter, driver, ticket clerk etc., because in the customers' experience these men and women *are* the railway. When they increasingly feel responsible, then many other problems take care of themselves. This is also true for the Church where we give so much time to discussing shared ministry. All Christians without differentiation inevitably share a common responsibility for the Gospel. But there is also a different sort of responsibility which derives largely from people outside the Church as much as within. There laity and clergy are not interchangeable, but they are deployable. When that is grasped, then each group and each person becomes more confident in their role.

2 We must discover places where the work is done when boundaries are fluid. There are problems and difficulties facing the Church today, but they are not peculiar to it. Most, if not all, institutions are in difficulty. In such a setting a lively body must stay alert to and concentrate on the fluidity of its boundaries in order to interpret the interchange with its environment and its inner life coherently and effectively. To do this we need at the diocesan and parochial level a stronger and less negative view of the Church as an institution. In any body which is made up of people and whose task is principally handling people's unconscious feelings, a continuing problem is how to get hold of empathic feelings and then use them. A strength of working at this in an institutional perspective is that such response to what is being required of us do not necessarily emerge where you would expect them. In a hospital, for instance, key evidence for the treatment programme may be discovered in the experiences of the nurses rather than the doctors, or in the way that different sub-groups are functioning with each other. The question always is how we can shift from dismissing these as by-products of institutional life (which is regarded pejoratively) and seeing them as important evidence of what we are doing. The same

applies to churches. So long as we think of these as gatherings of like-minded people, we shall lose vital information about what the Church is doing, where it is in the minds of people, and I would hazard, evidence about what God is doing. We need to be able to think strategically, not for the organization's sake as such, but so that we can keep at the theological and pastoral task of rightly perceiving the activity of God, and so indicating it to ourselves and others.

3 We need the resources to do both these things. And there is sufficient theoretical and practical evidence that to do this we probably still need churches and vicars. A parochial system enables the Church to stay in touch with, and hopefully engage, this range of incomprehensible feelings. It also provides people outside the church's membership with access points of opportunity, which is the most that we can expect. And it provides those who put themselves in the way of this work, clergy in particular, but also congregations, with a means of staying sane by directing them consistently to reality. This is not to confirm the status quo: that can always be questioned. Nor is it a dependent longing expressed nostalgically for days that never were — a priest in every parish. This is a myth, albeit a powerful and persistent one. But rather we need these as an organized way of approaching change and interpreting it as new opportunity rather than an onslaught of uncontrolled hostility from somewhere which has to be resisted, whether by 'holding the thin blue line' or reorganizing the Church hurriedly into something unrecognizable to congregation and parishioners alike.

The ramifications are considerable. Our theology needs a thorough look; our training has to be directed to the critical point of reflection and interpretation; our fear of institutions has to be seen for what it is — displaced paranoid feelings. It sounds grim, but I am hopeful. *Society does need what the parish church should be attempting to do, and without society the Church could not even attempt to do it.* If we back down from there now, we may be sure that we shall have lost some aspect of God, to our loss and that of the world of which we have the privilege of being in our generation part.

11

Conversion to the World

John Taylor

The Church is always having to be recalled to its true task, and always at risk of putting itself rather than the world at the centre of the picture. God's primary concern is with the world; He invites humanity to join Him in exploring His new world. The Church is called as the body which points to what God is doing and goes on celebrating and thinking about His activity. For this it needs a space of its own, but this must be open to the community, since it is with the development of human community that it is concerned.

I believe that if you were to ask any diocesan bishop to specify carefully what it is that claims most of his time and effort and anxious thought, he would probably say it is the ceaseless struggle to get people everywhere, but especially church people, to make the mental shift from a false image and false expectations of the Church, to an image and an expectation that are spiritually and theologically true.

A fortnight before my consecration I wrote for the diocesan monthly journal: 'I am convinced that God is teaching our Church in these days how to recover the attitudes of a missionary situation, and our survival as an effective Church of the nation depends on our readiness to learn that lesson.'

After contrasting our assumption of a continuing Christendom with the buoyant acceptance of a minority status by the Churches of Africa and Asia, I went on to say: 'Do we want to belong to a worship club or to a movement . . . A club is a much more accurate description of the way many people think of their local church than we realize . . . The alternative is to be a movement, a mission, which exists not for itself but in order to bring a new element into the life of the world.' I went on, 'I don't wish to over-simplify, but I submit for your consideration as individual Christians or as members of a Parochial Church Council, these two models — worship club or missionary movement. Which do you really expect your church to be?'

So you can judge how warmly I welcome the contrast in the discussion paper between 'the associational church' and 'the communal church'. I wholly endorse the bias which this paper betrays in favour of its exposition of the communal church. I share its evident disapproval of the introverted associational church. And yet I feel the need, which I hinted at in that diocesan article eleven years ago, to look rather more critically at the models we are setting up, so as to avoid drawing our lines of distinction at the wrong points and therefore creating another fantasy of good and bad that will be just as misleading.

So we need to examine people's expectations sympathetically and critically: church members' expectations of their local church and its activities, and of their clergy; the incumbent's expectations of his church members and their officers; the expectations of the local community (group by group, because they are not all the same), towards the church and its ministers; and the expectations of all these categories towards the wider Church and the wider society. But, how do we decide at any particular time and in any given situation which of all these expectations are sound and which wrong-headed? By what criteria are we to judge?

I am always a little suspicious of my tendency to make theology the ultimate standard, for she is no longer the Queen of the Sciences and her oracles are sometimes no more than pious rationalization. So I am greatly reassured by the ringing conviction of the third paragraph of the paper where it says, 'We believe the fundamental *theological* issue underlying all this shift and confusion is God, His nature and His purpose. What is to be believed about God and His relation to the world? And within that relation, what vision does the Church have of its function? Stated in *sociological* rather than theological terms, the question is to do with how the Church manifests its task as an institution *of* society and *within* society.' In other words, we are to judge which of all the expectations within and around the Church are right and which are false, by reference to the true task and function of the Church within the purpose of God in His relation to the world. The crisis for the churches in the West arises from their uncertain, unclear perception of their task. The discussion paper goes on to say: 'This question [of the task] has become problematic because the context in which the Church exists is increasingly one of fragmentation.'

That is a theme near to my heart and I believe passionately that a most significant aspect of the Church's ministry of reconciliation and healing in society is the restoration of human community, and I shall revert to that. Nevertheless I want to assert as vigorously as I can that the crux of our predicament is the question of task, not of context.

I find it helpful to analyse any institution under these five headings that are common to all systems, namely:

Context or environment
Task
Technology or tools
Structure or organization
People or personnel.

When any institution or system has become settled, these five components are integrally compounded so that it is not possible for any one to be changed without affecting each of the other four and altering the balance of the whole. This does not mean that changes should never be deliberately undertaken, nor that change which comes unsought is necessarily disastrous. But an institution can best survive change, and flourish after it, when the interplay between these five components has been correctly understood, anticipated and augmented. For example, the introduction of new *technology* into an industry is likely to be calamitous unless the changes it is bound to bring to the relations between the people and the plant, and consequently to the *structures* of the enterprise, are openly faced and allowed for.

The re-ordering of the authority *structure* of a great hospital can be justified in terms of cost-effectiveness and yet prove wholly destructive unless those responsible have truly understood how the older hierarchy evolved as a delicately balanced support system to enable very young *people*, *i.e.* the workers, to endure exposure to profoundly disturbing experiences. That is what brought the old hospital system into being, largely unplanned. And if that understanding is first achieved and shared, then the risky change of balance may be undertaken with a fair degree of safety. Or, using the hospital again, great damage can be done to *personnel* and great confusion introduced into the *structure* and the *technology* if a largely unacknowledged change takes place in the Health Department's understanding of the *task* of the hospital so that the concentration of research facilities and specialization replaces the medical care of a community as the prior function. But if a reformulation of the task is clarified, shared and accepted and the implications of this for all the other components of the institution are anticipated and provided for, then such a change may be carried through, not only with goodwill, but even with a sense of continuity.

I believe that what has befallen the Western Churches is this. Over the course of many centuries great changes have occurred in the *structure* of the Church, other great changes in its social context, and following inevitably on these, further changes in the *tools* that the churches have devised for their task, and in the sort of *people* that have occupied the pews and officiated in the sanctuary.

For the most part all those successive changes have crept up upon the Church, sometimes welcomed, more often deplored, but very rarely analysed or fully understood in their total effect. One could not expect it to have been otherwise. But, because they have been involuntary and unplanned, these successive alterations of the context, or the structure, or the technology, or the people in the churches, have necessarily brought about a series of shifts in the Church's perception of its *task* and of God's relation with the world.

We would be well served by a thorough and scrupulous historical study of this element in Church history, but it is beyond my competence to attempt even a brief run through. I can only remind you of St Augustine's great re-assessment of God's purpose in human history which he set out in his magisterial *City of God* in face of the breaking-up of the Christian empire by the barbarian invaders; a new concept which continued to influence Christian thought for many centuries. Or I can remind you of the rise of Islam and the virtual disappearance of the Church from Asia, presenting Christian thought with the question of a vigorous new world faith, a question that all the crusades merely postponed to our own day. I need only mention the names of Benedict, or Charlemagne, Vasco de Gama, or Calvin or Wesley to recall other mutations in the Church's definition of its task within the purposes of God for the world.

Now, considered sociologically, this should cause neither surprise nor dismay. But, theologically speaking, it is absurd, and there's our problem. God's relation with the world is constant. His purpose for it does *not* fluctuate with every change in the weather of history. Consequently Christ's mandate to the Church must be the same yesterday, today and forever. It is for us to trim the sails of our structure, our technology, our personnel, so that, when the winds of circumstances shift to another quarter, we still remain on course as far as our task is concerned.

Now most Christians would affirm that. But they don't have the same course in mind. What makes the Church so odd among the many institutions of society is its members' lack of an agreed perception of its primary task. I may say that that is exactly the trouble with British industry also; certainly there are other institutions that have this problem. But none perhaps quite so acutely as the Church, because by definition our task is unchangeable and this is the Church's abiding weakness. If you doubt the truth of this, consider what almost always takes place when a local Council of Churches decides to initiate a joint 'Mission' to the neighbourhood: in no time the planning committee is embroiled in argument as to 'what we mean by mission'. That can go on till Doomsday. Moreover each group believes it is interpreting Scripture aright. To revert to my nautical metaphor, all are sure they are reading the chart correctly. And so it has been from the beginning, for this strange and disconcerting confusion is nothing new for the Church. The chart itself appears to have been plotted by human navigators with differing points of view!

This suggests that the Lord of the whole enterprise always intended it to have a greater degree of contingency than we like. His purpose for the world, His predeterminate counsel, stands in eternity, outside time. But within the time process He, and we with Him, are explorers. We are on our way to an undiscovered land, a new world; so we sail uncharted waters beneath unfamiliar stars, and there is no means of knowing the right direction except to stay with Him.

The Bible is given to us just as the Holy Spirit is, in order that we may know God, and know Him in Jesus Christ, and it doesn't serve us particularly well if we look to it for other sorts of information, such as, 'Where are we going?', or 'How should we behave?' The only certain answer to, 'Where are we going?' is 'To the Father'; and the only clear counsel for 'How should we behave?' is 'Like your Father' − or so Jesus thought. And that drives us back to the Bible and to the illumination of the Holy Spirit in order that we may know our God more truly.

If God, within the time-space continuum, is fulfilling His eternal will for the world through a ceaseless exploration in which He invites the world to participate, then it should no longer bewilder us to find each generation perceiving the purpose of God afresh in the light of its own experience, for in fact that purpose can be perceived only at the point of intersection where the eternal love of God fills the transient 'now' of our existence. This means that we have to do our best to discover the purpose, and the Church's task within it, by clarifying our vision of God through our meditation on the Scriptures in the light of our contemporary experience. But, knowing that our best is only relative, we should be saved from the arrogance of insisting that our interpretation supersedes all previous ones or is the only tenable view for our own day. Such modesty, if we could achieve it, might even enable Christians to speak credibly at last about their 'common' task.

As far as my limited perception can judge, then, the Bible clearly affirms that God created and sustains the world out of love for the world and not as the raw material from which to gather the Church. On the contrary the Church, both of the Old Testament and the New, was called into being simply in order that through it, 'all the nations of the earth should be blessed.' God sent His son to save the world, not merely the Church, and God was in Christ reconciling not single individuals but the world, the cosmos, to Himself. So I have no hesitation in opting for a style of local church life with the community and not merely the congregation as the object of its concern. But I welcome the 'second thoughts,' if that is what they are, of the supplementary paper, for the original used at one point some very inadequate words to describe the task of the communal church. 'Its major concern,' says that paper, 'is to identify ways in which to show the community that it cares and is open to be approached by people about any issues which concern the health of the members of the community at large' (p. 7 above). What are we, a Citizens Advice Bureau? Now of course I realize that the Core Group that wrote the paper did not offer those words as a considered definition of the Church's task. And I am not going to chip away at them on that. I am not seriously questioning the use of these words at this point. But I think it may be helpful to ask why they are incomplete and what we should put in their place.

If I may revert to the image I used earlier, I would say that God invites the whole of humanity to share in His exploration of a new world. The Church is simply those members of the expedition who know the one who is leading it. And, as I said, to know Him is all there is to know about the object of our journey or the way to get there. Isn't that what Jesus said to Philip in the upper room? The Church is not the super-star of the caring professions, nor do we claim any special expertise. All we are called to offer is the insight into what a human community might become and the way in which it might achieve this which we derive from our relationship with God in Christ. I repeat that, all we are called to offer is the insight into what a human community might become and the way in which it might achieve this *which we derive from our relationship with God in Christ*. The service we give may be outwardly indistinguishable from that of others and we shall often find ourselves bettered by strange fellow-workers, but what makes an act Christian is its derivation, overt or implicit, from the nature of God. In His Body, the Church, Christ is still saying: 'The Son can do nothing of himself but what He sees the Father doing; for whatever He does, this the Son does in the same way.'

In this sense the Church's service of the world is always witness — it says something about God that is not generally recognized. And in so doing (and only in so doing) it often reveals something about the human community and its true reality which has also not been generally recognized. Doesn't this sum up the peculiarly Christian contribution of the Church, whether it be to the struggle in South Africa or the recovery of the inner cities of Britain, or the comfort of a family where a child has died. This is what Bonhoeffer was saying in his great posthumous work, *Ethics*. He says:

It is precisely this disordered world that in Christ is reconciled to God and now possesses its final and true reality not in the devil but in Christ. The world is not divided between Christ and the devil but, whether it recognizes it or not, it is solely and entirely the world of Christ. The world is to be called to this, its reality in Christ, and in this way the false reality will be destroyed which it believes that it possesses in itself as in the devil.[1]

Clergy and laity together, then, should work continuously to establish in their own minds and their own actions that conversion to the world whereby the congregation takes up its responsibility for mission to the community of which it is a part. The best way to start the process of any conversion is in practice — some change that is within reach, not too daunting, but which becomes a rubicon for those who make it, and causes them furiously to think where they are going. That is why John the Baptist talked about sharing food with those who haven't got it or making do with your pay if you are a soldier. The talking and the thinking can come later; realization of the meaning of it all comes later; but nothing happens if you start with talk. You have to *do* it: this is what the Communists are always saying. It is in practice not in theory that you realize the breakthrough truth.

And so a beginning can be made in such a simple way as deciding to let the Church Hall be used for a playgroup, lunch club and other community activities; or, better still, deciding to go shares with the Village Hall rather than building a separate Church Hall. It may happen with the decision to start a community paper for distribution to everybody instead of a parish magazine. It may start when the meetings of any residents' association are announced at church services and members encouraged to attend them. It may start with the letting of church premises for use by adherents of another faith who live as a minority group in the neighbourhood, and this can be a powerful witness to the courtesy of Christ who saluted other people's recognition of God without compromising his own truth. Actions such as these raise all the questions that educate us into fuller insight, and we can never come to the end of that education.

Let me give you a very recent experience of my own. In the last year of my time as Bishop of Winchester I was invited by our young twenty-one year old gardener and his twenty-one year old wife, with my wife, to go to the baptism of their son. This took place in a small local church in Winchester and most of their two families came up from Eastleigh, which was their home, and attended what was obviously for them a fairly unfamiliar service. But it was taken beautifully by one of the local incumbents. He called all the children who were there to gather around in front so they could stare and see what was going on, and they formed an attractive-looking group up there for everybody else to enjoy, and there was a great deal of participation, and it was beautifully conducted. We sat in the congregation and thoroughly enjoyed it. After the service we were walking home, my wife and I, and I said, 'Don't you think we should drop in at the tea-party in their home in the gardener's cottage?' And my wife, who is very sensible about these things, said, 'Well, you know we haven't actually been invited, there was no mention of it, we don't want to embarrass them all and I think it's probably a family occasion'. And I concurred, so we went home. The next day we met our gardener in the garden and chatted to him about how nice the service had been and he said, 'Oh, it was lovely to see you, though we were sorry that you didn't come to the party.' I tried to explain, but realized that we had made a big mistake, and perhaps hurt him a bit, although he was sweet about it.

That made me go back and think. For him the drinking of the champagne and the cutting of the cake were just as much a part of the ritual as the sprinkling of the water. That was for him a rather strange part, he could understand the rest. The point was that the Church has always assumed that Baptism is *its* ritual which it can dispense to those who seem to be qualified for it, but which it certainly has to explain. I came to see that what we are asked to perform is *their* ritual, and if we are prepared to do that as one of the still surviving rituals of our society, then we can claim the right to say, 'can we tell you what *we* see in this?' and to explain the deeper Christian understanding of that ritual. But I believe that unless we start with the re-acceptance of it as their ritual, we have very little chance of conveying the Christian interpretation of it. And I think that the same modesty applies to all the rites of passage which may still take place — the marriage, the funeral, and others.

In the same section of his book from which I have already quoted, Bonhoeffer insists that the Church is entitled to its 'space' but is not in the business of expanding its space at the expense of the world. It needs only sufficient space of its own for 'witness and serious thought'. That space for serious thought is absolutely essential if the Church is to witness in the sense in which I am using that term. We Christians are called to think about God and His purpose for this world which He has reconciled to Himself, in order that we may see the human community of which we are members as He sees it, and so help it to fulfil its true reality in Christ and to be what it really is. This is the voyage of discovery in which our only source of direction is our knowledge of the God who is leading us. This is the way in which it is right to fulfil the expectations that people have of the associational church. We need the withdrawal, the nurture, the dependency whereby we enter into profounder knowledge of God. Our wounds need healing and our inner resources renewed. But the Church must regain the insight of all the great masters of prayer that there is no true polarization between communion with God and sharing in His purpose for the world. In all deep intercession the vision of God and the vision of humanity flow the one into the other. For this thinking about God and His relation to the world we need the corporate declarations of our worship and also the more intimate and concentrated study in smaller groups. This is the Church's space where faith is overt and unashamed, but the worship and the study must be open to the community, and the contribution of those who choose to come into our space without sharing its presuppositions should always be welcomed, for it is precisely this to which we are charged to call them. 'Come and talk with us, if you will, about our understanding of God and what that says for unemployment, for this particular section of the city, for the problems of the falling-away of youth in rural areas.'

Involvement in the struggle to discern and realize God's good purposes in the community will very soon raise all sorts of questions about the nature of human affiliations. What gives a place a discernible identity? Why is it important for human beings to belong somewhere? Is it a factor in being truly human, and therefore an essential part of God's purpose for a reconciled world? How then should a local church relate to all those who professionally or as amateurs are working to re-create or sustain a sense of community?

It doesn't matter very much where an eclectic, associational church is sited and its parish boundaries are insignificant. But it is of the utmost importance that the area of responsibility of a communal church should coincide with a real unit of human community, be it a village or a group of villages that really feel they belong to each other, or a country town, or one of those neighbourhood villages into which most of our older cities are subdivided.

But we also have to be responsible about the circles within circles that are the common pattern of city and even rural life, and not allow a false attachment to some smaller unit to divert our concern for the larger whole which actually affects the lives of its citizens for better or worse. We saw this in Southampton, where there still is a tendency to concentrate on the particular suburb, the particular area, the particular place-name which make up a growing city. But what can the community of Thornhill do about the educational system of Southampton? What can the local community in Maybush have to say about the fact that 90 per cent of the employees in Southampton are working in one way or another for armaments? For that kind of question, which is still central to the humanity of the people there, it's the whole of Southampton that is the unit. That is why we cannot allow the separate parishes to remain isolated without, at the same time, going through the gruelling and exacting discipline of looking at Southampton together and allowing some of those isolating parish boundaries to be lowered in order that there can be common discourse and common planning.

And, moreover, in this day of extreme mobility, the Church has to consider the several communities to which an individual belongs for different departments of his or her daily life. Bonhoeffer talks about the world belonging wholly to Christ and in no way to the devil. Remember the devil's name is 'Legion,' multiplicity. Christ's name is 'Son of Man': man in his totality, his full humanity. That's our concern. That's what we have to look at and so we must be concerned with more than one community. This is where we strike sparks off those busy businessmen up in London making or breaking human lives in the decisions they take there, and who every weekend come back to a delightful ivy-covered church in a little village, which alone they choose to call 'my community'.

The Church has to be active at both ends of the commuter line, and has to make the commuters aware that it is at both ends, and that its message must concern the activities of both ends and their implications. Most people belong in more than one society, and in all the communities in which they belong, the work ones as well as the residential ones, there should be a church witnessing for God's perception of what they are doing and His purpose for that industry, for that Insurance Agency, for that Department of Government in which they spend so much of their time and are associated.

I don't want in any way to imply a finality in what I have to say, but rather to leave the road open for your further exploration of it. And so in T.S. Eliot's words I say to you, yes, as Church people, but far more as human beings, 'Not fare well, but fare forward, voyagers[2].'

PART III

12

The English Parish Church?: Concluding Reflections

The Core Group

The reader who has persevered this far may be wondering where the series of essays has been leading. That was the experience of many who attended the seminars, heard the essays as they were read and took part in the subsequent discussion. After the expenditure of all the time and energy, what were the conclusions? Did anyone significantly change what they thought as a result? Had there been any significant mapping of new territory, or was the exploration merely an interesting pub-crawl? In this chapter, we address those questions, though we choose to follow a route which in itself is a chart of the progress of the seminars.

In Chapter 1, the discussion paper, we used the psychological concept of projection to outline what we suggested were different ways in which churches respond to the world in which they are set. What is interesting is that the 'communal' understanding has frequently been interpreted as a flight to the past, as a desire to return to an idea of Christendom, which even if it once was helpful, is no longer so. It seems that there appears to be no way of understanding the relationship of a local church and its community in communal terms that does not sound quaint, even antique.

In exploring the whole area of 'communal' and 'associational' during these seminars, we were continually made aware of the absence of any commonly-held assumptions about what society is or what it ought to be. Even to use the word 'society' in this way can be felt to beg questions, as if the very idea of some common boundary in the mind, relating what I feel and do to what others feel and do, within a framework of shared if unspoken meanings, were no longer available as a way of understanding my relatedness to others, of informing vision and measuring reality. It would not be difficult to chart the reasons for this historically, and many would welcome the change on the grounds that a 'commonly-held assumption' is often a device used by the powerful to bolster a status quo which denies the rights of the powerless. But the significance of the change is that it is very difficult for me to discuss with you the rightness or otherwise of a particular opinion about society, because I cannot give you objective reasons why I hold my opinion that leave you free to determine whether or not you agree. We cannot find anything to which we can both appeal and so all I can do is to try to manipulate you into rejecting your belief and accepting mine. I may shout, cajole, bully or seduce, but the truth remains, 'society' has dissolved as a usable concept. We are left stranded as individuals. [1]

In any discussion, it is very easy to assume that 'communal' and 'associational' are used to describe competing ecclesiological ideologies, whereas beneath the understandings denoted by those two words there is a profound disagreement over whether the idea of society itself is worth trying to understand and work for. The assumption underlying one answer to the question 'Does Society still need the Parish Church?' is that if society is not to disintegrate further into a series of fragments, each competing shrilly with the others, then someone, or some people, must somewhere be prepared to cling onto the very idea of society. That is, that there is some notion of what a human community can become, some over-arching source of values through which people can explore their relatedness to each other and to their environment. The 'communal' model, whether or not it is actualized in the traditional parish church of the Church of England, offers an understanding of the Church as a place where the idea of society can be explored.

The evidence seems to show that the modern church no longer believes in society, but is content to be one of many competing fragments. We interpret this to mean that the modern church no longer believes in a God for whom the 'world' is the primary focus of love, but rather believes in a God who has abandoned the world in favour of a select few. If this church sees itself as so separated from the world that the world becomes the representation of the devil, that all this church has to offer society is a means of escape from that world, then of course society has no need of it. But the evidence that is available to the church that people in society do still need it is dismissed as 'mere folk religion'. Of course, the New Testament offers clear evidence that from the earliest days 'world' was understood ambivalently. It seems to be used both as a description of that which God loves and as a description of that which resists God, stands over and against God. But both understandings are vital, and if the modern church is determined to focus on only one, then the church is an obstacle to belief in God, not a means to belief in God. 'We find it hard to believe that God loves the *world* and has saved the world. We find it hard to think that God actually created all the world of secular activity and has a design for it, intends it to reflect his glory, does not automatically regard it as sinful and simply shot through with evil, for which there is any hope by some sort of cauterisation or immunisation.'[2]

The evidence for this trend towards one understanding only of God's relation with the world is plentiful. The church seems more and more to think that it owns the means of grace, demanding that everyone fully understands its own definition of the sacraments. It forgets that the sacraments belong, not to the church, but to God. By misappropriating the sacraments in this way, it prevents people from exploring their relatedness to the source of their values. For example, by demanding that people attend marriage preparation courses addressed by endless doctors or bank managers, the Church hinders them from exploring at a profound level what the marriage vows expressed in the rite really confront them with.

Another piece of evidence lies in the way in which the church forgets that the origin of the word 'parish' is 'one who lives beside', the neighbour, often meaning the alien or the stranger.

So, the 'parish church' sees everyone as neighbour, not just as potential converts, and is therefore able to represent them before God and to represent God before them.

The Church refuses to take its context seriously, refuses to explore the meaning of 'locality', but instead insists that there is a standard, often New Testament, model of the church that can be applied in every situation. So the most important people become those who are members.

Church people don't really believe in the Church with its ineffectiveness, its limitations and shortcomings, which it seeks the grace of God to overcome so that it will do God's will. They set out to make it more effective so that they can believe in it, because unless it becomes more effective it will not be credible, literally, able to be believed in. And, not believing in the Church, the Church does not believe in its worship of God. It prefers to make worship into a celebration of togetherness or membership, understandable by all, rather than a celebration of the mystery of God and the disclosure of what it means to be a human being.

In so far as the Church does all these things, it has ceased to believe in a society, *i.e.* that we human beings associate together. If it has ceased to believe in society then society has no need of it, and will give it no authority. Such a church may well continue as a sect, and will have successfully saved its life — but will have lost it.

Need

Another way of exploring the difference between the communal and the associational is by exploring the distinction between 'being in need' and 'having needs'. It may be that by asking the original question in the seminars, 'Does society still need the parish church?' we colluded with an assumption that the Christian faith exists to answer the needs of society. Behind that is an assumption that human beings are essentially people who have got needs, air, food, shelter, love or whatever. A human being is almost defined as someone having a need met by someone else. So everything is valued to the extent that it is able to meet those various needs, and the value of the Church to society is that it is able to meet the totality of humankind's needs. So the success of the Church is measured in much the same way as the success of the supermarket. Do people come? Does it make a profit? Indeed, many of the plans to reorganize the Church are made in order to achieve just that degree of success.

But the primary fact is not that human beings have needs, but that they are in need because they are contingent beings. To be in need is to be dependent, and when human beings recognize the real nature of their situation, they are led to acknowledge that there is a dependent relation between themselves and their environment. 'No man is an island, entire of itself; every man is a piece of the Continent, a part of the main' (John Donne). Human beings need to consider how to behave so as to utilize this being in need, their dependent condition, as a means for their growth and development as persons, both individually and corporately. It is in seeking to relate to the environment that humans can struggle to find the values of what it means to be a human being. Some do not know how, or choose not to, do this. They experience the dependent relation to the environment as denigrating or as a cause of their impotence. They therefore manipulate the situation by denying the dependence; they lie, steal, destroy, enslave. They treat the satisfaction of various needs as the end of a human being, whereas it is in reality the means whereby a human being discovers her or his true end. As they do this, they also sever the human/divine relation, an activity the Bible calls sin. The first eleven chapters of Genesis chronicle in vivid detail the consequences for humankind of failing to acknowledge its dependence, of seeking independence from the source of its being, its Creator. The stories of Genesis find an echo in the claim for human autonomy made at the time of the Enlightenment, when the chains of the oppressive claims of religion were broken so that human beings could be free to forge their own destiny. It may well have been true that the claims of religion were oppressive; but out with the bath-water of a warped religious system which itself was seeking to deny its dependent condition went the baby of the acknowledgement that the ultimate human condition is dependence. So dependence has come to have a derogatory meaning, describing a state of infancy that is grown out of. The wish is to be independent, not to need the various props that serve to bolster the weak or immature.

We do not accept that dependence is a state to be grown out of: rather, a state to grow into. What human beings require in order that they can grow and develop is some safe way of being able to regress and get in touch with their feelings of dependence, their 'being in need'. Only then can they explore their relatedness to their source of values, reassess them in the light of their experience and reinternalize them in preparation for the task of living them out in their various activities, at work, at home, at leisure, in the community etc. Our thesis is that society needs some institution to handle this on behalf of the society, to be openly concerned with the relatedness of society to its values. In England, the Church has traditionally been that institution where people in society can express their feelings of what it is to be 'in need'. This may be a peculiarly English phenomenon, indeed even a peculiarly Anglican phenomenon.

A communal church will be marked by its willingness to accept this role in society. It will see itself in worship as human beings in need presenting themselves to God, and doing this *on behalf of* society, representing all human beings in need. It will therefore accept that many will use it as a focus for their feelings of dependence, as a place where things are not unpredictable, where their feelings of pain and bewilderment, awe and joy, (feelings most frequently engendered at times of birth, marriage, sickness and death), will be accepted and handled with care and sensitivity. It will also accept that many will use it only on those occasions, but it will not feel angered or hurt by that, content that it can be a channel of God's grace merely by being there, dependable, competently managing the boundaries between life and death, health and sickness, the known and the unknown. It will therefore feel used, even abused, and its members will willingly accept that role in the conviction that they are doing something valuable. But that is not the full message of the Gospel. The danger is that a church will merely foster superstition if it is not always in its worship offering up its own values and those of its community for judgement and reordering in the light of what it discerns is God's will in Christ. The liturgy spells it out, grace, repentance, redemption and new life. The attitude is captured by the words of the confessor. 'Go, your sins have been forgiven. Pray for me, a sinner.' Such a church is needed by society, as has been discussed above: but such a church also needs society, for without it, it lives only for itself.

An associational church seems to see its role more in terms of meeting the needs of people. People come to have their needs met, and the representative function is less important. So, an associational church is less than comfortable when asked to handle society's need to express its dependence. It does not regard its context as of primary importance; indeed people may come to it from far and wide, frequently because the local church does not answer their needs for one reason or another.

This is not to say that the communal church is 'better than' the associational. Frequently, a communal church becomes indistinguishable from a shrine for folk religion, becoming totally assimilated to the beliefs of the society that surrounds it. That is why one of the crucial contexts to be considered is the ecclesiastical. It may be that a particular church is able to operate communally, to handle the dependent needs of its community and run the risk of becoming merely a shrine, because there is an associational church nearby. Similarly, a particular church can operate associationally because there is a communal church nearby. The two churches need each other. Such an understanding would give substance to the claim that 'we are members of one another' and would undermine an ecumenism which seeks an inclusive church of unmitigated sameness. It would also avoid the false polarization between communal and associational which leads to fruitless competition, and lead to a potentially fruitful exploration of the relationship between the two.

Institution and Body of Christ

Another way of looking at the tension between communal and associational is by seeing it as a function of two ways in which church people conceive of the Church. In one way, they see themselves as voluntary members of an institution, concerned to see, as we have already pointed out, that the institution meets their own needs and requirements. They are concerned that it has an organization that ensures its future health and vitality; they are equally concerned that a proper place is given to the expression of personal faith. In another way, church people see themselves as baptized members of the Body of Christ, commissioned through that baptism to share in the priesthood of Christ, that is, to function in the world as human-beings-of-the-new-creation. They see themselves in the world as human beings with other human beings, working with and serving them in their situation. As we have already outlined, this tension is fundamentally a theological one, but it can be seen most clearly in terms of time. An institution, particularly a voluntary one, requires members who are committed to spending a great deal of time in supporting and maintaining it. It needs leaders and helpers both to provide appropriate structures in which the young can be taught, outsiders contacted, newcomers welcomed and lapsed members followed-up, and to ensure that the organization can be held together, its committees serviced and its buildings maintained. The beginnings of such an organization can be seen emerging in the Early Church in the Book of the Acts, as membership grew to what were becoming overwhelming proportions. On the other hand, if members are going to be involved in the world, functioning as what we describe as 'universal priests', that is also going to demand a great deal of time and commitment. To be involved in all the doings of a local community, working to influence it in ways which enable it to express more fully the will of God for the world, to join caring organizations of various kinds, to participate in local political activity and to be concerned with the wider issues in society and the world, leaves little room for active participation in the organization of the local church. In fact, such persons, perhaps seen at only one act of worship a week, may well be accused of a lack of commitment, whereas they see their primary vocation as baptized Christians not in the institution of the church but in exercising their priestly role in the world.

We might say in relation to this distinction between the institution and the Body of Christ, that in the associational model the institutional membership is more important than the functioning of the world, whereas in the communal model it is the other way round. (In very rare cases is this distinction exclusive: it is rather a question of relative importance.)

So, in the associational model, the more like-minded the congregation, the more effective the church action is likely to be. There will be a tendency therefore to attract people of a similar background and belief; newcomers will be assimilated to a common pattern of behaviour. There will be close working relationships established within a tight organizational pattern, and those who do not fit in will find themselves excluded. Such a congregation will not be related to its geographical location, but will attract members from a wide area, all of whom will be looking for an institution that will answer their needs for support, both at a personal level and for their spiritual growth. In the communal model, because the focus is on the complexity of the world and its human problems, the more varied the membership is, the better. As the Body of Christ, members relate to and work in the world as it is around them, and so there is a tendency for the work of maintaining the institution to be left to a few. For this sort of church, the geographical location gives them both an actual neighbourhood for which they can accept responsibility and, because of the parish boundary, a definition and therefore necessary limitation of the extent of their formal responsibility. In worship they seek to offer their world to God in prayer and praise, representing the world to God and God to the world.

There is also a difference in the relation between clergy and laity. In the associational model, the roles of clergy and laity are not experienced as static or hierarchical in the literal sense. Rather the clergy seek to share their role with other (lay) leaders and welcome support in the common task of administering and leading the institution. In many cases, the roles of clergy and laity are interchangeable, so that there is pressure, in the Church of England, for lay presidency at the Eucharist. In the communal model, the roles of clergy and laity are significant in that for the laity to be the 'universal priesthood', they need the constant support and building up by the ordained priesthood. 'Shared ministry' on this understanding does not mean an interchange-ability of role, but that both clergy and laity have their own roles, both of which are vital. So the clergy may have the responsibility for worship, seeing it as a way in which the 'universal priesthood' can be resourced for its ministry in the world. Equally, the laity have a responsibility to bring that world to worship, so that the worship can be resourced by their ministry in the world.

In practice, as local churches are *both* institutions *and*, if they are being true to their calling, the Body of Christ, these two models overlap. The different denominations and their individual local churches express a variety of combinations of these two models. Some of these combinations exhibit acute tension between different members of the same congregation, between clergy and people, and between people and people. Again we want to stress that one model is not better than another. Within the total economy of the Church of God both are required. The significance of a visible, vigorous, institutional church is that it represents the group that believes, and no group can function without the necessary organization to enable it. However, a vigorous institution which does not see itself as committed to the world in which it is set, not because the world offers potential new members but because it is that world that it seeks to influence in conformity with God's will, is living solely for itself. It is, of course, often the paid leaders of the institution who feel the resultant tension most keenly. Somehow a way of understanding how to live with that tension creatively must be offered.

Now You See It, Now You Don't

Thus far we have been arguing as though what we were working with were two kinds of church. A church is *either* communal *or* associational; a church is either an institution or the Body of Christ. In the course of the seminars, it was very difficult to avoid getting into a position where the claims of one were exalted above the claims of the other.

But there will always be a tension felt between what the Church is for, and what it is actually doing. The aims of the Church are glorious and all-embracing, however they are expressed, but the experience of many church members is that the Church never lives up to those aims. How, for example, can a local church reconcile the fact that it exists to bear witness to the revelation of God in Christ with the fact that much of the agenda of the church council or its equivalent seems to be taken up with money and drains? How is it that an institution that ought to be outward-looking spends so much of its time on its own affairs? How is it that a group of people committed to the command to love each other should spend quite so much time in engaging in petty squabbles?

We suggest that the way out of this apparently depressing situation is to see that we are not working with two kinds of church, one of which is better than the other, but with the same church looked at in different ways. What we are talking about are two ways of looking at the Church, two ways of thinking about it.

Any church must see itself in terms of purpose and intentionality, always be concerned with its primary aim. It will set itself aims and objectives, and decide the best way of organizing itself so as to achieve them. It will be very concerned with its boundaries and what goes on within those boundaries. Leadership will consist of managing those boundaries effectively, and whoever happens to have the particular skills required can exercise that leadership. So someone skilled in financial matters can be asked to monitor the financial affairs of the church; another, skilled in pastoral care, can be asked to organize the caring within the church. But essentially the focus will be on what is going on within the institution, and the effort will be put into maintaining it and helping it to grow.

But there is another way of seeing the Church that does not have to do with purpose. It will see the Church as part of the larger whole that is society, with a complex pattern of rules and relationships that do not seem to be *for* anything; they just are. That is to see the Church, not in terms of what it aims to be, but as it really is with all the resistance to change that drives many to despair, with all its weaknesses and failures. It just is, and week by week it meets with all its brokenness simply to offer that to God, for the brokenness is that of the world in which it is set. That is all it can do. It receives whatever is brought to it, holding it, accepting it, in what seems an endless cycle which never gets anywhere.

These are not two different churches, but two ways of looking at the same church, two ways of picturing it in the mind. Both are true, but neither can be subsumed under the other. So the experience is of 'now you see it, now you don't', as the two ways alternatively slip in and out of focus. If, instead of trying to be aware of both ways, a local church allows itself to think in only one way, then it will fall into one of two traps. The first of these is to cut itself off from its context, to see the world as a place to flee from, to suggest by its attitudes and behaviour that it is not concerned with society at all. The second is to lose touch with its purpose so that it is incapable of doing anything more than just exist, accepting without challenge the assumptions that all and sundry project onto it.

Somehow it has to struggle to incarnate in itself both the purpose of what God would have it be and the present reality of what it perceives itself to be. It has to believe itself to be the earthen vessel that contains the treasure about God, believe that God loves it for what it is and not for what it could or should be. It will understand that it does not exist to get things right, but to struggle to interpret the human experience of being broken and fallible within the purpose of God for the world. In that struggle it can enable those who come to it to interpret for themselves what it means to be a human being who is broken and fallible. Seen in that way, the Church will enable the members of the community that it serves to get in touch with a source of values which is not just dependent on the community itself.

This could be immensely releasing, for by holding these two ways of thinking together, Church people would be putting together parts of themselves. They would both be able to sense the wholeness of everything, the inter-connectedness of the created order, and see themselves as a part of that whole, and be able to make sense of what appears to be the mundane business of raising money for the church roof. They would see that the Church is called to be the earthly Body of Christ, the Word incarnate in a particular place in a particular time.

Where Now?

If there were, as a result of this exploration, clear practical conclusions, then there would have been no need of the exploration. For if it were possible to prescribe certain actions which would guarantee that the Church could be more effective, then those actions would have been taken already. The Church has had much experience of seeking such actions, centuries of it.

What is clear as a result of this exploration is that there are certain ways in which people can think about the relation of the Church and society that will result in new ways of behaving that could, in turn, have profound consequences both for society and for the Church. We cannot predict what those new ways of behaving will be, or what the consequences will be, but that there will be a shift is certain. For if one part of the whole thinks in a new way, then other parts change, not in the predictable ways of cause and effect, but because that is the way things are.

Those ways of thinking can be described, even if the resultant behaviour cannot be predicted. They can be summed up by saying that people will think 'parish church'. That is not to say that people will carry around the traditional picture, but that they will willingly take on the responsibilities of being a 'royal priesthood', of seeing themselves as responsible to God for their society, praying for and offering up the world in which they live and work as being that world that God loves. They will also see themselves as responsible to their society for God, accepting that they will be asked to hold and work with society's need to get in touch with its dependence. As representatives of God, they will not reject this need for they will share it, nor will they work with it only on their terms. Furthermore, they will be and do all this as human beings, meeting others as human beings, for that is what God has called his earth creatures, women and men, to be. They will believe in and work for the possibility of a society that can repent of its sin and acknowledge its dependence on a source outside itself, a society that will epitomize the proper functioning between humans, God and the world. By acknowledging that dependent relation, human beings will be able to develop as persons in relation to their environment, that is, they will love God and their neighbour.

Notes and References

PART I

1   1   Newbigin, L., *The Other Side of 1984*, World Council of Churches, 1983.
           Tiller, J., *A Strategy for the Church's Ministry*, CIO Publishing, London 1983.

PART II

4   1   McLeod, H., *Religion and the Working Class in Nineteenth Century Britain*, Macmillan, London 1984.
    2   cf Yeo, S., *Religion and Voluntary Association in Crisis*, Croom Helm, London 1976, where the author describes the relationship of Huntley and Palmer in Reading, to the local parks, libraries and churches, Non-Conformist and Anglican in the town, and how this collaboration between local churches and local firms collapsed in the late 19th and early 20th century.

6   1   Quick, O.C., *Essays in Orthodoxy*, Macmillan, London 1916.

2   Oppenheimer, H., 'Missions, morals and Folk Religion', in P. Turner, and F. Sugeno, *Crossroads are for Meeting*, American SPCK, USA 1986.

3   Coleman, P., 'A Local Temple', *Theology*, LXXXVIII, (1985), p. 424

4   Kerr, P., 'Playing Away', *Theology*, LXXXVIII, (1985), pp. 374-382.

7   1   Dyson, A., in *All are Called: Towards a Theology of the Laity*, CIO Publishing, London 1985.

10   1   Turquet, P., 'Leadership: the Individual and the Group', in G.S. Gibbard, J.J. Hartman, and R.D. Mann, *Analysis of Groups*, Jossey-Bass, USA 1974.

2   Hay, D., *Exploring Inner Space*, Penguin Books, London 1982.

3   Martin, B., *A Sociology of Contemporary Cultural Change*, Blackwell, Oxford 1981.

4   Bettelheim, B., *The Informed Heart*, Penguin Books, London 1986.

11   1   Bonhoeffer, D., *Ethics*, SCM Press, London 1955.

2   Eliot, T.S., 'The Dry Salvages', in *Four Quartets*, Faber and Faber, London 1944.

PART III

12   1   For a discussion of this dilemma, see *After Virtue* by Alasdair MacIntyre, Duckworth, 1981.

2   Geoffrey Paul, *A Pattern of Faith*, Churchman Publishing, 1985 p. 142.

Select Bibliography

Bowker, J., *Licensed Insanities*, Darton, Longman and Todd, London 1987

Brierley, P., *UK Christian Handbook 1983*, Bible Society, London 1983

Carr, W., *The Priestlike Task*, SPCK, London 1985

Carr, W., *Brief Encounters*, SPCK, London 1985

Currie, R., Gilbert, A. and Horsley, L., *Churches and Church Goers: Patterns of Church Growth in the British Isles since 1700*, Clarendon Press, Oxford 1977

Gilbert, A., *The Making of Post-Christian Britain*, Hutchinson, London 1980

Habgood, J., *Church and Nation in a Secular Age*, Darton, Longman and Todd, London 1983

James, E., (ed.) *Stewards of the Mysteries of God*, Darton, Longman and Todd, London 1979

Martin, B., *A Sociology of Contemporary Cultural Change*, Blackwell, Oxford 1981

Martin, D., *Breaking the Image*, Blackwell, Oxford 1980

Martin, D. and Martin, B. *Religious and Cultural Change in Britain*, Blackwell, Oxford 1987

McLeod, H., *Religion and the Working Class in Nineteenth Century Britain*, Macmillan, London 1984

Moltmann, J., *The Crucified God*, SCM, London 1974

Moyser, G., *Church and Politics Today: The Role of the Church of England in Contemporary Politics*, T & T Clark, Edinburgh 1985

Newbigin, L., *The Other Side of 1984*, World Council of Churches, 1983

Newbigin, L., *Foolishness to the Greeks*, SPCK, London 1986

Oppenheimer, H., *The Hope of Happiness*, SCM, London 1983

Reed, B.D., *The Dynamics of Religion*, Darton, Longman & Todd, London 1978

Selby, P., *Liberating God*, SPCK, London 1983

Shaw, G., *The Cost of Authority*, SCM, London 1983

Tiller, J., *A Strategy for the Church's Ministry*, CIO Publishing, London 1983

Tiller, J. and Burchall, M., *The Gospel Community*, Marshall Pickering, London 1986

Turner, P., and Sugeno, F. (eds.) *Crossroads are for Meeting*, SPCK, USA 1986

Welsby, P., *A History of the Church of England 1945–1980*, Oxford University Press, Oxford 1984

Yeo, S., *Religion and Voluntary Association in Crisis*, Croom Helm, London 1976

The Contributors

Lesslie Newbigin

Formerly a Bishop of the Church of South India and then Lecturer at the Selly Oak Colleges. Currently Minister at Winson Green United Reformed Church. Author of various publications including *The Other Side of 1984*, and *Foolishness to the Greeks*.

David Martin

Professor of Sociology at the London School of Economics and Political Science, and Honorary Assistant Priest at Guildford Cathedral. Author of several books including *The Breaking of the Image*, *Religious Vision and Political Constraint*, with Bernice Martin, *Religious and Cultural Change in Britain*.

Clifford Longley

Journalist. Joined *The Times* in 1967, Religious Affairs Correspondent from 1972 to present day.

Helen Oppenheimer

Formerly lectured in Christian Ethics at Cuddesdon Theological College. Member of Inter-Anglican Theological and Doctrinal Commission. Author of several books including: *The Hope of Happiness*, and *The Character of Christian Morality*; and has contributed to symposia, including *Stewards of the Mysteries of God*.

Ruth Etchells

Formerly Head of Aigburth High School for Girls in Liverpool, and then senior lecturer and residential tutor in Chester College of Education. Went to Durham in 1968 as residential tutor in a new University College (Trevelyan) before being appointed to St John's College with Cranmer College in 1978 as its first woman Principal.

John Tiller

Formerly Chief Secretary of the Advisory Council for the Church's Ministry and now Chancellor of Hereford Cathedral. Author of *A Strategy for the Church's Ministry*, and, with M. Burchall, *The Gospel Community*.

Peter Selby

Bishop of Kingston since November 1984, previously Canon Missioner in the Diocese of Newcastle. Author of *Look for the Living — the Corporate Nature of Resurrection Faith*, and *Liberating God — Private Care and Public Struggle*.

Wesley Carr

Dean of Bristol since 1987, formerly Canon Residentiary, Chelmsford Cathedral. Involved in research, consultancy and training in the churches and other institutions. Author of *The Priestlike Task — A Model for Developing and Training the Church's Ministry* and *Brief Encounters — Ministry through the Occasional Offices*.

John Taylor

Bishop of Winchester between 1975 and 1985 and, before that, General Secretary of the Church Missionary Society. Author of *The Go—Between God*, *Enough is Enough*, and other books.

Members of the Core Group

David Armstrong	Consultant, The Grubb Institute
Paul Bates	Director of Training, Diocese of Winchester (Convenor)
Giles Ecclestone	Vicar of Over, Cambridgeshire
Jean Hutton	Director, Centre for Explorations in Social Concern of The Grubb Institute
Bruce Reed	Executive Chairman, The Grubb Institute

The Grubb Institute

The Grubb Institute was founded in 1969 as an independent applied social research organization, with charitable status. It engages in research, advisory work and training in the fields of social and organizational analysis.

The Institute works collaboratively with a wide variety of organizations and agencies, both in the UK and overseas. Its scientific staff come from different disciplines and professions and have particular experience of the systemic approach to issues concerning individuals and the groups, organizations and communities to which they belong.

From its foundation the Institute has had a special commitment to the study of religion. The staff have wide experience of work with churches, religious orders and Christian organizations representing different denominations, both in this country and the United States. *The Dynamics of Religion*, (Bruce Reed 1978) presented a theory of religious behaviour and its significance for the well-being of society, which sought to bring together social, psychological and theological frames of reference for understanding the life and practice of churches. Subsequent work has aimed to extend and develop this approach and its practical application to the work of clergy and laity in the contexts of British and American society today.

Centre for Explorations in Social Concern

The Centre is a unit of The Grubb Institute, set up in 1984 with the help of the Joseph Rowntree Memorial Trust.

The aim of the Centre is to be a base for people from different sectors of national life, who are concerned to accept responsibility for changes taking place in society. The intention is that in providing the stimulus and conditions for people to work with each other in the exploration of current social concerns, the Centre can be a catalyst for developing a new vision of how they can influence the direction in which society is moving.